Pan Breakthrough Books

Pan Breakthrough Books open the door to successful self-education. The series provides essential knowledge using the most modern self-study techniques.

Expert authors have produced clear explanatory texts on business subjects to meet the particular needs of people at work and of those studying for relevant examinations.

A highly effective learning pattern, enabling readers to measure progress step-by-step, has been devised for Breakthrough Books by the National Extension College, Britain's leading specialists in home study.

Margaret Attwood is senior lecturer in industrial relations and personnel management at the Anglian Regional Management Centre. Before entering higher education, she worked as a personnel specialist in the electronics industry. As well as teaching personnel specialists and line managers on qualification courses, she undertakes a wide range of consultancy work and in-company programmes. Currently a major interest is the development of equal opportunities programmes. She is a member of the panel of independent experts designated by the Advisory, Conciliation and Arbitration Service to deal with claims for 'equal pay for work of equal value'.

Pan Breakthrough Books

Other books in the series

Pan Breakthrough Books

Introduction to Personnel Management

Margaret Attwood

A Pan Original
Pan Books   London and Sydney

First published 1985 by Pan Books Ltd
Cavaye Place, London SW10 9PG
9 8 7 6 5 4 3 2 1
© Margaret Attwood 1985
ISBN 0 330 28590 4
Printed and bound in Great Britain by
Richard Clay (The Chaucer Press) Ltd, Bungay, Suffolk

If you wish to study the subject-matter of this book in more depth, write
to the National Extension College, 18 Brooklands Avenue, Cambridge
CB2 2HN, for a free copy of the Breakthrough Business Courses leaflet.
This gives deails of the extra exercises and professional postal
tuition which are available.

Contents

Introduction

As employees or potential employees, the management of people at work concerns all of us. Often there seems to be more mismanagement of employees than there should be. Unfortunatley it is not easy to generate easy prescriptions for effective personnel management. What appears to encourage high productivity in some situations may not work elsewhere. Nor can we copy from other nations. At one time everything American was thought likely to lead to an industrial utopia. Now we seem as intent to learn from the Japanese. This book is no panacea for all ills. Personnel management is a lonely business. Stuck somewhere between management on the one hand and employees on the other, the personnel specialist must examine the particular circumstances of his own organisation and establish those methods for managing employees, which will work best there.

This book examines the process of managing people at work as practised both by the personnel practitioner and the line manager. My aim is to provide both established practitioners and students with some thoughts and guidance on the subject, whilst emphasising that effectiveness in this function of management is not just about memorising a few aphorisms. After all, a little knowledge is a dangerous thing!

Whilst writing this book, I have learnt the difficulty of attempting to compress a large area of knowledge into a relatively small amount of text. Of necessity I have made decisions about the emphasis which should be given to particular aspects of personnel management. Without doubt these reflect my own experiences and values.

How to use this book

As a management teacher, I have come to believe that practising managers and other students benefit most from the opportunity to practise newly acquired knowledge and skills. Ideally they should be able to integrate these with their own experience. Therefore, three types of exercise are built into the text.

Activities Here you are encouraged to try out areas of personnel management practice, particularly by questioning employees, personnel specialists and line managers. There is emphasis on the value of undertaking these activities in your own organisation, or, in one known to you, allowing you to compare techniques and cases described here with the reality of personnel management in your experience. Unfortunately there are not always answers to these activities since human behaviour and organisational practice vary. This knowledge should give you the confidence to try to learn from your own experience and to develop your own skills.

Self-checks These are questions which give you more immediate feedback on your understanding of ideas developed in the text.

Reviews It is important that you try to consolidate your learning. Here you are given the opportunity to recall ideas and information developed earlier in the book.

A friend read a draft of part of this book and commented that she liked the idea of these self-study exercises but that they would be no good for lazy people like her! Of course, whether you take the trouble to work through them systematically is up to you!

Acknowledgements

Daily contact with colleagues past and present, and with personnel specialists and line managers, has provided the material for this book. They are too numerous to mention but I owe a debt of gratitude to them all. Patrick Hare wrote the lion's share of Chapter 2, 'Planning for people', and encouraged me to embark on this project. Brigid van Bruggen cast her lawyer's eye over the employment legislation chapters. Don Rumble, Carole Taylor and Mick White gave me the benefit of their experiences of personnel management. Lastly my thanks to my family – Bill, Abi and Jonathan – for putting up with me whilst I toiled!

Note

I have used the conventional masculine gender 'he' for 'he and she' throughout this book. No discrimination is implied.

1 | Definitions of personnel management

Personnel management is that part of management concerned with the management of people at work. However, like many things in life, reality is more complicated. In this introductory chapter, we shall attempt some initial definitions:

- Most organisations have a specialist personnel department which gives support to managers and supervisors, who have direct responsibility for the management of people.
- A wide range of people – personnel specialists, line managers and supervisors – practise personnel management.
- There are a number of specialist management techniques which together comprise personnel management.
- The practice of personnel management varies greatly from one organisation to another.

This chapter examines each of these four points. By the end you should have a general awareness of the nature and complexity of personnel management and of some of the reasons for this.

The structure and organisation of a personnel department

The function of a personnel department is to assist with the acquisition, development and retention of the human resources necessary for the success of the organisation. It is unhelpful to imply that there is one best design for a personnel department. Here we look at some options.

Activity

Is there a personnel department in the organisation in

1

which you work? (If you are not working at present you can answer this for an organisation with which you are familiar.) To whom does the most senior personnel executive report?

Most organisations now have a specialist personnel department. Increasingly this is likely to be headed by a member of the board of directors.

Self-check

Will the task of the personnel department in encouraging the effective management of the organisation's employees be easier or harder if its head is a member of the board of directors?

It should be easier in that its head will have access to the chief executive. By being involved in board-level decision-making, the chief personnel executive should be able to ensure that personnel policies and strategies support corporate goals.

Within the structure shown in figure 1 the *personnel director* would have responsibility for:

- Formulating the organisation's personnel policies and overseeing their implementation by both members of his department and other managers.
- Advice to other board members on personnel matters.
- Management of the personnel department.

The *industrial relations adviser* would be likely to carry responsibility for:

- Formulating industrial relations policies in conjunction with the personnel director.
- The provision of advice, guidance and information to the divisional personnel managers (and, through them, to other managers) on industrial relations.
- Guidance to all managers on employment legislation.

Depending on the structure of industrial relations in the company, there might also be an advisory or an executive role in trade union negotiations.

The *group manpower development adviser* would be responsible for:

- The formulation of policies for the development of the organisation's human resources, in conjunction with the personnel director.
- Advice, guidance and information to the divisional personnel managers (and, through them, to other managers and employees) on training and development.

The divisional personnel managers would provide a day-to-day personnel service covering all aspects of personnel management, industrial relations and manpower development, for their division. It would also be necessary for them to provide information to the personnel director and the advisers to allow policies to be formulated and monitored satisfactorily for the organisation as a whole.

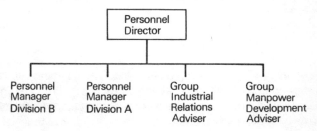

Figure 1. Organisation structure for a personnel department

Activity

At the beginning of this chapter you were asked whether your organisation has a specialist personnel department. As explained there, the odds are that it does. What are the roles carried out by the specialist staff in the department? Draw a small organisation chart as shown in figure 1.

There are, of course, no right or wrong answers here. The specialisms which exist within a personnel department will depend upon such characteristics of the organisation as:

- size;
- profitability;
- status of the personnel function;
- nature of the market for the organisation's products;
- nature of the labour force from which workers are recruited.

We could add to the list, but an example should help demonstrate how such characteristics influence the structure and organisation of the personnel function. In the national newspaper industry, union power historically has been based on the pressure of daily production deadlines. The unions control many activities undertaken by personnel specialists elsewhere. An example is recruitment and selection where management contacts the union when a job is vacant. Personnel specialists tend to concentrate on industrial relations.

Activity

Look at the job advertisements in a journal such as *Personnel Management*. List three specialist personnel jobs which you find there.

My three were:

- Grading officer for the head office of a public authority employing over 700 manual and white collar staff. The job is concerned with the operation of a job evaluation scheme in which employee representatives, as well as line managers, are involved.
- Management trainer to join a team of seven in the management development unit of a large building society. The unit provides a wide range of training and development activities for the society.
- Graduate recruitment officer to coordinate the graduate recruitment programme for a large pharmaceutical company.

Your list may differ from this, since there is now a plethora of personnel specialisms. All the personnel activities covered by this book may be carried out by specialist personnel staff or by generalists, whose work covers the whole range of personnel, training and industrial relations activities for a department or a whole organisation.

In small companies there may be no specialist personnel department, or, where one exists, it may be staffed by a single employee with responsibility for everything from visiting sick staff to the provision of safety goggles.

Detailed organisation of the personnel function cannot be prescribed easily. However, if personnel management activities are to be effectively carried out, it is important that line managers feel that their immediate needs are being met, as well as that attention is being given to longer-term matters. If the personnel specialist finds that longer-term considerations are constantly relegated to the bottom of the filing tray, one can safely assume that something is wrong!

Who practices personnel management?

The Institute of Personnel Management stresses that personnel management 'forms part of every manager's job as well as being the particular concern of the specialist'.

Personnel roles and responsibilities

In practice the specialist role may take a number of forms:

- audit;
- executive;
- facilitator;
- consultancy;
- service.

The audit role

Personnel specialists have responsibility for ensuring that all members of management carry out those parts of their roles concerned with the effective use of human resources.

The executive role

Personnel management is part of every manager's job, but some personnel activities are carried out by specialists rather than by line managers or supervisors. Factors which seem to influence the division of responsibilities include potential economies of scale if the activity is carried out by specialists, the need for 'expert' knowledge, organisational tradition and the preferences of both specialists and line managers. For example, it seems that personnel specialists tend to maintain a high profile in those areas of work which they see as most important and prestigious. Industrial relations falls into this category.

The facilitator role

Many personnel management activities require considerable skills and knowledge if they are to be carried out effectively. One of the responsibilities of personnel specialists is to see that those who practise such activities, as part of a more general managerial role, are equipped to do so. Attempts by personnel practitioners to carry out this task may lead to conflict between themselves and line managers.

The consultancy role

Managers may confront a variety of problems as they attempt to supervise employees. These may include motivation difficulties, lack of training or pay grievances. The individual manager may meet a particular problem infrequently and, therefore, may need advice in order to resolve it successfully. In this area the role of the personnel specialist can be equated with that of an internal management consultant.

The service role

Managers need information on which to base decisions about the deployment of their staff. The personnel specialist can provide, for example, statistics on pay rates nationally, by industry or by occupation. Because of the increase in complexity of employment legislation, there is often a need for information on the interpretation of such laws by the courts as well as the detail of the law itself.

Activity

Talk to members of the personnel department in your own organisation or one with which you are familiar. Seek information on the roles they are fulfilling in their efforts to support managers and supervisors. Can you categorise their roles in the way that I have suggested above?

You may have found this difficult since my categorisation of the work of the personnel specialist is not definitive. There will be overlap in particular cases between roles. For example, in the area of advice on employment legislation, there will often be little distinction between 'service' and 'consultancy'. At times one role will assume greater significance at the expense of others; for example in a recession, pressure on indirect costs, of which a personnel department is one, may restrict the more creative aspects of the work of specialists, in particular those which here I have labelled, 'facilitator' and 'consultancy'. It is false to assume that personnel specialists should always operate in one particular way. Far better that those involved in personnel management recognise the potential variations in the specialist role and can diagnose what might be the optimum division of labour between specialists and line managers.

Self-check

Below are listed a number of activities often carried out by personnel specialists. Into which category – audit, executive, facilitator, consultancy, service – does each fall?

1 Negotiating the introduction of a new job evaluation scheme with trade union representatives.
2 Running a workshop for managers on the skills of performance-appraisal interviewing.
3 Checking that annual performance appraisal interviews have been carried out.
4 Discussing possible ways of improving a problem employee's attendance and timekeeping with his manager.
5 Compiling and circulating labour turnover statistics to departmental managers.

   6 Interviewing applicants for jobs in the computer department with the departmental manager.

ANSWERS

1 Executive.
2 Facilitator.
3 Audit.
4 Consultancy.
5 Service.
6 A combination of consultancy and service, i.e. helping line managers to reach selection decisions and providing information on conditions of employment, etc. There may also be elements of the facilitator role. Pre-selection planning and post-interview discussion may provide the specialist with an opportunity to give managers informal feedback or guidance on the use of selection techniques, such as questioning skills.

Universal good practice in personnel management – a myth for students or a reality for practitioners?

Personnel management's central concern is the efficient utilisation of one of the resources available to organisations: its employees. In this way, it can be equated with other functions of management – finance, production or marketing.

Self-check

From our discussion so far, would you agree that personnel management is simply a collection of people-management techniques which can be used in all organisations?

If you remembered our discussion of the characteristics of an organisation which influence the specialisms which exist within the personnel function, your answer would have been 'no'. It would be convenient if you could simply lift a tome from a shelf to get the answers to all problems of dealing with employees. Unfortunately, although there are books which purport to provide such answers, there is little universal 'good practice' in this area of management. Techniques which appear to assist in the effective utilisation of manpower in one organisation may fail elsewhere. For example, where a company has a history of strikes, employees may react with hostility to managerial proposals on new working practices; where industrial peace has been the norm for years, and relationships between management and workers have been good, there probably would be much less distrust of identical proposals. No universal principles govern the formulation of personnel policies and techniques. However, there are certain basic headings and guidelines which together may be said to compromise personnel management.

Activity

Talk to anyone who occupies a specialist personnel role or who manages staff in an organisation which employs more than 500 people. Ask them to list six personnel management responsibilities. These may be either the responsibility of a specialist department, or of managers and supervisors, or both.

What did they say? Probably the list would include the following:

- recruitment and selection;
- training;
- performance appraisal;
- wage and salary systems and administration;
- industrial relations;
- welfare and counselling.

The Institute of Personnel Management has answered the question more eloquently by saying that personnel management is that part of the management process concerned with:

recruiting and selecting people; training and developing them for their work; ensuring that their payment and conditions of employment are appropriate, where necessary negotiating such terms of employment with trade unions, advising on healthy and appropriate working conditions; the organisation of people at work, and the encouragement of relations between management and work people.

You should have learnt from the activity that, no matter what the organisational context, it is always necessary for someone to have responsibility for the movement of people into, through and out of an organisation, if the human resource is to be effectively managed. However, the detailed organisation of such responsibilities, for example between managers or supervisors and specialists, and the specific techniques utilised will differ from organisation to organisation. This passage of people through organisations is the integrating theme of this book.

Is personnel management a profession?

Personnel specialists have sought to become recognised as professional in the same way as members of other professions – law, medicine and accountancy, for example.

In the UK, much of this debate has centred around the role of the Institute of Personnel Management (IPM), which has developed a rigorous and lengthy training scheme for entry to membership. Does this mean, therefore, that personnel specialists are professionals? Sociologists have examined the process by which occupational groups achieve professional status. A quotation will help us:

Professionalisation might be defined as a process by which an organised occupation, usually but not always by virtue of making a claim to special esoteric competence and to concern for the equality of its work and its benefits to society, obtains the exclusive right to perform a particular kind of work, control, training for and access to it, and control the right of determining and evaluating the way the work is performed.*

How does the work undertaken by personnel specialists measure up to such yardsticks of professionalism?

Firstly, personnel management is not the exclusive preserve of personnel specialists. It is undertaken by most managers as part of their role in managing employees. Personnel specialists do not exercise autonomy over their own work, which is determined for them by more senior management within the general framework of corporate goals. Personnel specialists may feel that they occupy the role of 'piggy in the middle', caught between the

* E. Freidson, *The Professions and Their Prospects*, London, 1973.

organisational goals of profit or efficiency and the needs of employees. However, when there is redundancy there is usually no doubt that the personnel specialist is part of the management team and must assist other managers in the efficient running of the organisation.

Secondly, the IPM's examination scheme, though well accepted both in industry and in higher education, does not regulate entry to the occupation in the way that medical, legal or accountancy training does. Indeed many personnel practitioners are not members of the IPM. A reasonable conclusion is that personnel management is not a profession; rather it has become a well-developed function of management.

Review

Which of these statements are true or false?

1 Personnel management is only undertaken by trained specialists. *True or false?*
2 There are textbooks which will tell intending personnel specialists or line managers everything they need to know about techniques, which will lead to effective human resources utilisation in their own organisation. *True or false?*
3 It is possible to define personnel management under a number of broad headings concerned with the management of working people. *True or false?*
4 Though its status as a profession is in doubt, personnel management is a well-developed function of management. *True or false?*
5 There is no one best design for the organisation structure of a personnel department. *True or false?*

ANSWERS

1 False.
2 False.
3 True.
4 True.
5 True.

2 | Planning for people in organisations

The focus of this chapter is the techniques available to plan the process whereby people enter, move through and leave organisations, in accordance with the overall business objectives. Management's choice of a manpower strategy will depend on the values held by those in positions of power within the organisation. In most private-sector companies employment policies are usually geared to corporate goals of profit and growth. Here the planning of human resources becomes a search for those individuals who now and in the future will contribute most to the success of the organisation. By contrast some local authorities are developing equal opportunities policies and practices. These have considerable implications for the planning of manpower in that they aim, over time, for the population of the organisation to come to resemble that of the local community which the authority serves.

What is manpower planning?

A number of techniques have been developed to help managers answer the question, 'How many staff do we need both now and in the future?' These are variously termed 'manpower planning', 'manpower budgeting' and 'human resources management'. By the end of this chapter you should be able to explain the main stages of manpower planning and should have an awareness also of the role of the personnel department in this.

Activity

Colin's Cars is a successful manufacturer of sports cars. Firstly list five factors which influence the demand for labour by the company. Secondly list five factors which influence the supply of labour to the company.

Your lists should have included some or all of the following:

Factors influencing the demand for labour
- The objectives of the company and its future plans.
- Market demand for the company's sports cars.
- The technology used by the company.
- The product range or numbers of models produced.
- The productivity per employee.
- The degree to which components are 'bought in'.
- The level of stock.

Factors influencing the supply of labour
- Company policies in so far as they affect recruitment and selection, manning levels, retirement and redundancy.
- The attractiveness of jobs in the company including pay and other terms and conditions of employment.
- The skills available in the labour market.
- Union agreements, for example on manning levels.
- Government legislation, for example on employees' rights.

Self-check

Why is the attractiveness of jobs in the company an important influence on the supply of labour?

The numbers of people who can be persuaded to work for Colin's Cars will be influenced by the nature of the work and the terms and conditions of employment offered as compared with those in competitor organisations. The rate at which existing employees leave the company will be influenced by similar factors.

We would need to know more about Colin's Cars and the state of the local and national economy to undertake a detailed manpower planning exercise for the company. However, the company's demand for labour will be determined predominantly by the demand for its products. By contrast the demand for the services of the National Health Service can be considered to be almost infinite. Here available labour resources are predominantly determined by national government funding. On the supply side some factors influencing the number of people available for work are short-term in character – the numbers of people currently seeking employment in the locality, for example; others are much more long-term – changes in the birthrate or retirement age, for example.

Self-check

Can management control all the factors affecting the demand for and supply of labour?

No. They cannot control the birthrate, for example! Most companies also cannot control the demand for their goods, nor can they control government policies. However, many large companies do attempt to influence government thinking. The cigarette manufacturers, for example, have successfully lobbied government to prevent major reductions in product demand by restrictions on smoking. Manpower planning attempts to analyse likely influences on the supply of and demand for manpower with a view to maximising the organisation's future performance.

Manpower planning – a summary

The planning of manpower, then, involves trying to obtain:

- the right people
- in the right numbers
- with the right knowledge, skills and experience
- in the right jobs
- in the right place
- at the right time
- at the right cost.

It can be seen as an attempt to balance the demand for employees with the numbers available. However, it is not merely a 'numbers exercise' concerned with the *quantity* of manpower; it also involves issues related to the *quality* of manpower such as the requirements for training and development.

The process of manpower planning involves a distinct number of stages, which are shown in figure 2.

Although the stages of the manpower planning process are

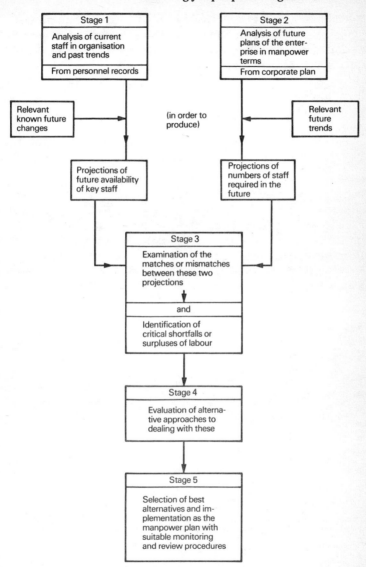

Figure 2. The manpower planning process

shown in sequence in the diagram, stages 1 and 2, which involve an analysis of the organisation's past and present manpower on the one hand, and the corporate or business plan on the other, generally are undertaken in parallel. Other stages occur in sequence since each depends on adequate operation of the previous part of the process.

Stage 1. Analysis of current staff in the organisation and past trends

Activity

What do you think are the 'key facts' you need to know about manpower in an organisation in order to begin the process of manpower planning? If you are working you should find it useful to ask your personnel department what information it keeps for this purpose.

Your list should have included some or all of the following:

The numbers of people employed by
- grade;
- job type, title or department;
- sex;
- age;
- length of service;
- skill or educational level.

Also you would need statistics about the utilisation of manpower including the rate of labour turnover, the working hours lost due to sickness or absence, the rate at which people are promoted and the productivity per person employed. It would also be useful to be able to look at the way that these statistics have changed over the recent past.

Having collected this information we need to begin to analyse its implications. One way of doing this is to present it in aggregate form using simple histograms. This is often done, for example, to analyse the age distribution of employees.

Analysis of employees' age distribution

Self-check

Figure 3 shows the age distribution of pilots in Senior Airways in 1984. Pilots normally retire at fifty-five. Examine the percentage of staff retiring in each year (scale 2). What is the problem for Senior Airways?

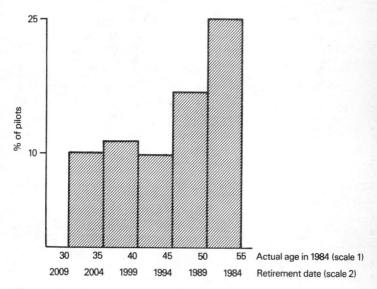

Figure 3. Age distribution of pilots in Senior Airways 1984

You should have been able to see that, in the following five years, 25 per cent of the pilots will retire. Since it costs over £500,000 to train a pilot, the company has a serious problem.

So age distributions can tell us something of problems due to retirements in the near future. An imbalance in the age structure also would exist if many people in senior positions were young.

Self-check

What are the manpower implications of this?

The promotion prospects of more junior staff would be very limited. They might leave or become very demoralised.

Analysis of length of service

The analysis of length of service also gives insights into the processes which underlie decisions by individuals to leave jobs or to stay in them.

Self-check

Figure 4 depicts the length of service of middle managers in Colin's Cars. From the graph you can see that middle managers are relatively new to their jobs. Why should this be a potential threat to the success of the company?

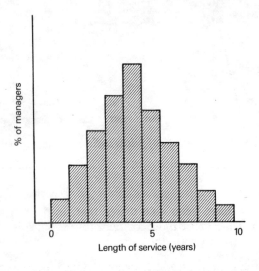

Figure 4. Length of service of middle managers in Colin's Cars

Many researchers believe that it takes two to five years to become really effective in a managerial job. If a lot of managers are still learning to do their jobs, it is unlikely that their department will be as effective as those with more experienced managers.

Analysis of labour turnover

If we analyse the behaviour of leavers in an organisation then we find that the shape of the length-of-service distribution for leavers (called the 'completed length of service' or CLS) takes the same shape in almost all cases.

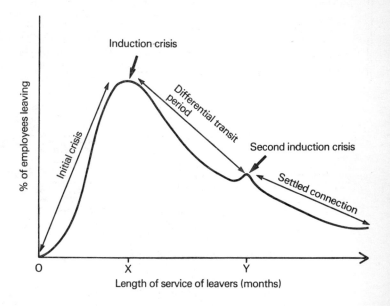

Figure 5. The process of labour turnover

Soon after the day on which the individual joins the organisation, there comes an 'induction crisis'. The new employee asks himself, 'Oh dear! What have I done?' And his supervisor or management may say, 'We've recruited the wrong person for the job.' At this point, depending on a number of factors such as the availability of jobs elsewhere, the new employee may decide to leave.

The induction crisis occurs anything from one month to two years after engagement, depending on such variables as the nature of the job and the organisation. If there is no severance, a period of mutual accommodation and adjustment goes on. Both management and the employee modify their expectations of the other. This period is given the term 'differential transit'.

A *second* induction crisis may occur from two to five years after the date of engagement. (It is often very small and sometimes may not occur at all.) In other words, after there has been mutual accommodation, there may still be feelings of concern. The new employee may express this as, 'There's no future here', whilst management may be saying, 'He really has not turned out as well as we hoped.' If this second induction crisis – the small peak – is surmounted, then the final period of 'settled connection' takes place during which the individual is much less likely to leave.

It is interesting to note that similar-shaped curves are obtained for most jobs or organisations, although the exact positions of 'X' and 'Y' in figure 5 vary for particular organisations and jobs.

Other measures of labour turnover

Labour turnover index Many companies use index measures of labour turnover, which express the number of leavers or 'stayers' as a percentage of those employed.

The labour turnover index is defined as:

$$\frac{\text{Number of leavers in a time period}}{\text{average number employed during the period}} \times 100.$$

More accurately this might be referred to as an index of labour wastage since it is concerned only with the process whereby employees leave the organisation (wastage) and not with the leaving process and subsequent recruitment (turnover). You should also note that the choice of time period is left to the user.

(A year or a month is common.) The average number employed is usually the average of those employed at the end, i.e.

average number employed =

$$\frac{\text{number employed at start of period} + \text{number employed at end of period}}{2}$$

Self-check

Lyttlewood Enterprises has 2,350 employees at the beginning of January and 2,450 at the beginning of February. During January 725 people left. What is the average number of people employed by the company in January?

Average number employed = $(2,350 + 2,450) \div 2 = 2,400$.

Self-check

What is the turnover index for January?

Index = number of leavers ÷ average number employed = 725 ÷ 2,400 x 100 = 30.2 per cent. Thus the labour turnover index was 30.2 per cent for January for Lyttlewood Enterprises. This should give management much cause for concern unless of course it has prompted employees to leave because of redundancy or early retirement.

Labour stability index Another index focuses on the stability of labour. The labour stability index is defined as:

$$\frac{\text{number of staff with more than} \times \text{periods of service}}{\text{number employed} \times \text{periods ago}} \times 100.$$

It is customary to use this index for periods of one year.

Self-check

Hill Engineering have 250 staff of which 200 have more than one year's service. The business is contracting. One year ago they employed 300 people. To calculate the stability index, which figure would you put as the denominator of the equation?

The answer is 300 since that is the number of people employed one year ago.

|| Then using the formula given above, calculate the stability index.

Stability index = (200 ÷ 300) × 100 = 66.6 per cent.

Labour turnover and stability indices can be produced over time for any group of staff. You could choose to look at a particular department or factory, or at all the people employed on a certain job. The indices for such a group then can be monitored over time. Figure 6 shows a control chart which could be produced to monitor turnover. In this case it would be sensible to examine the reasons for the sudden and dramatic increase since October.

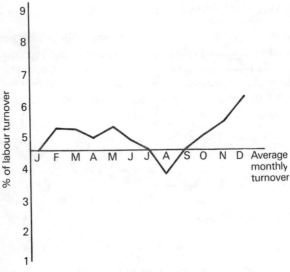

Figure 6. Control chart to monitor labour turnover

It is difficult to be certain of the causes of labour turnover. Often leavers are asked to complete a form giving their reasons for leaving, or an 'exit interview' is conducted. Psychologists have

suggested that different reasons than those which are given for
leaving cause people to look for other jobs. Figure 7 shows a 'step
model' for a sample leaver.

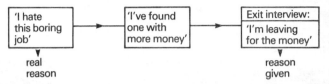

Figure 7. 'Step model' for a sample leaver

Self-check

In figure 7, what was the *real* reason which caused the
individual to look for another job? Was this the same
reason as was given at the exit interview?

Our sample employee found his job boring, and as a consequence looked for another job. He found one with better pay and
gave this as his reason for leaving.

Despite this complication, it is possible to analyse labour
turnover by reasons for leaving. There are some classifications,
which are helpful.

Activity

Ask two of your friends to give you their reasons for leaving
any jobs which they have had. Think about your reasons for
leaving jobs. Compile a list of ten reasons which may cause
people to leave jobs.

Your list should have included some or all of the following:

- dismissal;
- internal transfers (redeployment, promotion or demotion);
- death;
- sickness or ill-health;
- more money;
- more interesting work;

- pregnancy;
- domestic reasons (such as the move by a spouse to another area of the country);
- retirement;
- poor relations with a supervisor or workmates.

It is useful to see whether any patterns emerge amongst employees who leave.

Self-check

Suppose Hill Engineering lost three secretaries to Lyttle-wood Enterprises within six months. What questions should the managing director of Hill Engineering ask?

Obviously he should investigate the rival firm, asking: 'How can they attract my staff so easily? Is it that they are offering something better than us? Or are we not using staff properly?'

This comparison process is important. Comparisons can be made within a company as well as with other organisations.

Other analyses of manpower

Other analyses of manpower can help us monitor the results of employment policies. For example, in organisations where care is being taken to ensure that equal opportunities policies are put into practice, sex ratios by department or grade will be calculated, as will ratios which measure the proportion of employees from ethnic minority groups. Skills inventories can tell management about available staff skills, some of which may not be currently in use – for example, employees' use of foreign languages or computing skills.

Analysis of absenteeism and sickness using time-based ratios, such as:

- average number of days lost per year per employee, or
- number of spells of absence and their duration per year per employee:

can be used to identify both 'problem' employees and 'problem' jobs or departments (by comparison with the average).

It also will be useful to compute the total number of working days lost per year due to absence or sickness for departments and for the organisation as a whole. This statistic, if computed annually, provides a useful monitoring device, which can be used to help shape policy either to reduce absence levels or, at least, to plan levels of manning in such a way as to cause least disruption to services or production. It may seem odd to accept sickness or absence but, in many industries, rates are as high as 5 per cent daily. To ignore these would result in unproductive and costly bottlenecks.

Analysis of current staff and past trends – summary

Review

What is the aim of this analysis in stage 1 of the manpower planning process?

The aim is to evaluate how many and what kinds of staff will be available in the future. As a result a kind of manpower head-count budget can be produced, as shown in figure 8.

Social workers in post 1984	84	
Expected leavers 1984–85 (10%)		8
Retirements (early)		1
		—
		9
Net social workers available	75	
Sickness (5%)	4	
	—	
Staff available for work	71	
	—	

Figure 8. Manpower budget of social workers 1985

Stage 2. Analysis of the future plans of the enterprise in manpower terms

> *Review*
>
> Is it true to say that this stage of the manpower planning process cannot be carried out until stage 1 has been completed?

No. Remember, we said that stages 1 and 2 can be carried out in parallel with each other. Stage 2 is by far the more difficult stage of the process. At this point we need to ascertain:

- what the organisation's future plans are; and
- what these plans mean for the numbers of staff required to carry them out.

Here we are concerned with the corporate or long-range plans which set the scene for the organisation over a three- to five-year period. Many organisations have planning systems, while others improvise as they go along. All that is needed is some statement of work output in quantitative terms. For example:

- 'sales will be £1,000,000'; or
- 'outpatients will be 25,000 per annum'.

The difficulty of corporate planning is the main reason for the problems associated with this stage of manpower planning. Especially in a recession, corporate plans are likely to be volatile and changing. The manpower planner must translate this statement of workload into numbers of employees required. The easiest way of doing this is to assume that the relationship between the level of production and the number of people employed will remain roughly constant in the future.

Ratio-trend analysis

One manpower-demand planning method which uses this assumption is ratio-trend analysis. It involves the study of ratios which existed in the past between such factors as the number of direct and indirect workers or between the level of production in a particular department and the number of workers employed there.

Self-check

Is this an accurate method of forecasting future manpower requirements?

It is a crude, though sometimes useful, method. That is, the relationships measured may change in future. There may be economies of scale as output increases; technological change is likely to increase productivity per employee. Suppose a clerk can handle 500 inquiries per month and there are 2,500 each month. This suggests that five clerks would be employed. However, if you were computerising the system of dealing with inquiries, you might expect a 20 per cent increase in efficiency. This would mean that only four staff would be required. Such factors have to be considered carefully for each individual case.

Work study or organisation and methods (O & M) techniques in manpower-demand planning

A refinement of ratio-trend manpower-demand forecasting uses work study and organisation and methods techniques. The output or sales forecast is converted into a production schedule in the way suggested above. This is then broken down into department-by-department, function-by-function or job-by-job work schedules for the period concerned. From an analysis of the man-hour content of various tasks in the past and from data derived using work study, a forecast of the required manning levels for various job categories can be produced.

Often organisations have specialist O&M or work study departments which can gather the information needed to use this method of manpower-demand forecasting. The detail of these techniques is outside the scope of this book.

Generally the application of these techniques involves the collection of data about:

• the exact nature of the work being done;

- measurement of this work and examination of the methods used to seek improvements;
- comparison of work output between departments, and with other organisations where relevant.

Managerial judgement in manpower demand planning

It may be unrealistic to assume that the relationship between output or sales and the number of people employed will remain constant in the future.

> *Self-check*
>
> In your organisation, who might be able to guess with a reasonable degree of accuracy the number of people who will need to be employed on particular types of work in future?

The answer is probably managers directly responsible for that work. However, the use of this type of manpower-demand planning is not without dangers.

> *Self-check*
>
> Can you think what these are?

Managers may not be objective; some may be 'empire builders'; therefore the result could be overmanning. One useful method is for top management to prepare planning guidelines for departmental managers, possibly acting on the advice of personnel or O&M specialists. Managers can be told to think about some of the following:

- replacements for retirements, leavers, transfers and promotions;
- possible improvements in production;
- redeployment of existing manpower;
- planned changes in output levels;
- planned introduction of new methods and equipment;

- planned reorganisation of work;
- the impact of changes in employment law or collective agreements.

Review

In stage 2 of the manpower planning process, we have examined some methods of analysing the manpower implications of corporate plans. List three such methods.

ANSWER

- Ratio-trend analysis.
- Work study and O&M techniques.
- Managerial judgement.

Stage 3. Examination of the matches or mismatches between manpower-supply forecasts and manpower-demand forecasts and the identification of critical labour shortfalls or surpluses

The results of the two previous stages of manpower planning process can be represented in tabular form.

Job category: Porters	*1985*	*1986*	*1987*	*1988*
Estimated demand	25	30	35	40
Estimated supply	20	17	15	10
Difference	-5	-13	-20	-30

Figure 9. The difference between demand for and supply of hospital porters 1985–88.

We now will consider ways of dealing with the mismatches, considering the two cases – shortages and surpluses – separately.

Self-check

What two questions would you need to ask in order to decide whether or not a projected shortage of manpower was critical to the achievement of the corporate plan?

1 'Is the work undertaken by the staff who are likely to be in shortage critical to the organisation's future sucess?'
2 'Does the gap between supply and demand get wider or narrower as we get further into the future?

We can define 'critical skills' as follows:

- A skill or job where recruitment is expensive or difficult.
- A skill or job where training or retraining of existing staff is impractical or costly.
- A skill critical to the effective functioning of the organisation; for example, salesmen in insurance brokerage, or pilots in airlines.

Then we need to see whether there is a clear trend in the development of staff shortages; that is, whether the projections increase or decrease in a regular pattern each year. We also need to see whether the absolute magnitude of the numbers is striking. Generally this would be the case if the shortage or surplus was more than about 10 per cent of the total staff employed. In the example for the hospital porters the small numerical shortage is 20 per cent of the total number of porters employed and there is a clear trend. It is necessary to look at strategies to deal with such mismatches.

Here we have discussed an example of a labour shortage. All too often these days the results of manpower planning reveal that the organisation will have a future labour surplus.

Stage 4. Evaluating the options

Self-check

List the options you would consider if there are:

(a) too many staff in a given work area.
(b) too few staff in a given work area.

Compare your lists with the following.

Options if there are too many staff
- Natural wastage.
- Redundancy (voluntary and compulsory).
- Redeployment (including training, if needed).
- Early retirement.
- Dismissal.
- A freeze on future recruitment.
- Part-time working or job-sharing.
- Elimination of overtime.
- Move to more labour-intensive methods or new products.
- Search for additional or new work.

Options if there are too few staff
- Recruitment.
- Redeployment.
- Promotion or demotion.
- Extension of the contracts of those about to retire.
- Use of freelance, agency or temporary staff.
- Overtime.
- Productivity bargaining.
- Automation or the elimination of jobs.
- Increase capital investment to increase productivity (for example, by the introduction of new technology).

As you can see, there are a number of strategies to deal with each case of projected labour shortage or surplus. It is important to take into account the particular nature of the organisation, and of the environment in which it operates, before embarking on a strategy. Here is an extract from a document which evaluates the voluntary redundancy option where a future surplus of staff is projected. First the advantages of this strategy are assessed.

Voluntary redundancy – the options for Mike's Manufacturing

Advantages

Avoids compulsory redundancy.

Therefore should be acceptable to the trade unions (i.e. the company has a policy of 'no compulsory redundancy' with the recognised trade unions).

Will not subsequently damage the ability to recruit.

Voluntary redundancy agreement with trade unions already exists.

Therefore compensation payments for those who leave are already agreed.

Therefore scheme would be quick to set up and administer.

Likely that 5 to 10 per cent of staff will apply. This is within the target identified from the forecast of future staff surpluses.

Therefore this would give rapid reduction in wage costs.

Would allow some recruitment, when necessary.

No moral obligation to retrain or place staff who decide to volunteer for redundancy.

Before examining that part of the document which assesses the disadvantages of this strategy, here are a few comments on the use of the voluntary redundancy option. Many companies, when faced with surplus staff, use a strategy which combines natural wastage with a freeze on recruitment.

Self-check

If a freeze is placed on recruitment, turnover invariably falls. Why is this? (Look at the labour turnover section again.)

Labour turnover is highest during the early weeks and months after the date of engagement. Remember the 'induction crisis'! Hence, if no new staff are recruited, the turnover rate will fall dramatically.

Natural wastage together with a recruitment freeze may cause certain departments to suffer dramatically, and affect work capacity. Careful monitoring and control are necessary to manage the process.

The use of dismissal as a strategy for dealing with staff surpluses may seem an odd choice but overmanned companies often 'toughen up' on offenders as a means of reducing staff.

The move to labour-intensive methods may also seem strange, but one hi-fi manufacturer with surplus craftsmen modified a product to be hand-finished (raising the price accordingly) and thus improved productivity.

Taking on additional work is another ploy. A firm of travel agents introduced related services such as travel insurance and travel goods as a way of more effectively using staff.

Voluntary redundancy – the options for Mike's Manufacturing

Disadvantages

Only the good staff may decide to leave.

Some departments or units may be depleted.

Costly option, since agreed compensation payments are greater than those laid down in legislation. (See Chapter 15.)

It is not absolutely certain how attractive the scheme is to employees.

Difficulties of dealing with staff who volunteer for redundancy whom the company does not wish to lose.

Most of these points are self-explanatory. However, the option of raising retirement age (in selected cases) may need a little more discussion. An airline with pilot shortages did this, and obtained an average of three to five years' additional service from them. This gave a breathing space to train replacements.

Voluntary redundancy – the options for Mike's Manufacturing

Conclusions and recommendations

Invite applications from employees for discussion purposes and the collection of data. Then make a more rational decision, based on better information on 'take-up' and costs.

Examining the possible solution for organisational manpower problems and thinking them through clearly is a creative and exciting prospect, which often will pay real dividends for the time spent on it.

Activity

Which of the strategies listed and discussed in this section

do you feel would be most appropriate in your own organisation (or one of which you have some fairly detailed
knowledge)? Select one suitable strategy for a situation of
projected labour shortage and one for a labour surplus.
Repeat the advantages and disadvantages exercise, which
we did for the voluntary redundancy option in Mike's
Manufacturing, for your chosen options.

There is no right or wrong answer. What will work in practice will
depend on the nature of your organisation. It would be useful to
discuss your answer with someone with a good knowledge of the
present and future workings of the organisation.

Stage 5. Selection of best alternatives and implementation as the manpower plan with monitoring and review procedures

Now it should be possible to suggest the most likely strategies to
improve the manpower situation. These are incorporated into
the manpower plan and analysed and costed in more detail.
Clearly, however, all manpower planning is based on assumptions or estimates, which subsequently may prove wrong. Some
of the bad publicity for manpower planning has arisen because of
the failure to monitor trends, check assumptions and treat the
plan as a flexible document not as a 'tablet of stone'.

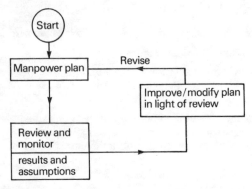

*Figure 10. Manpower planning – monitoring and review pro-
cedures*

The best way to consider a manpower plan is perhaps as a scenario or picture of what is felt to be likely to happen in the future based on the best evidence today. To operate without some kind of forward planning of manpower is at best risky and at worst destructive for the organisation in any kind of competitive or resource-limited environment.

Review

List the five stages of the manpower planning process.

Could you remember them? Good! Now try to apply these techniques to some real-life manpower problems. Good luck.

3 | Recruitment and selection

In this chapter we concentrate on the process of matching the characteristics of individuals to the demands of jobs. This is the purpose of recruitment and selection. As in other areas of personnel management you will find that unfortunately there are no easy prescriptions for success. Much depends on the knowledge and skills of those involved, whether line managers or personnel specialists. In addition, as you should recall from earlier in the book, any personnel technique needs to be relevant to and effective within the context of a particular organisation. Towards the end of the chapter you will be encouraged to examine how you might evaluate the effectiveness of recruitment and selection in an organisation.

How to start

> *Activity*
>
> Suppose you have opened a shop and have decided that you will need an assistant to help you. What general questions should you ask yourself before attempting to recruit someone to fill the position?

- What job do I want to be done?
- What kind of person do I think will do it most effectively?
- How can I find some people who might be suitable to fill the job?
- What methods should I use to decide which one would best fit my requirements?

These are the questions which this chapter tries to help you answer. In broad terms you should have realised that in order to fill in a job in any organisation you must follow a number of stages. These stages can be expressed as follows:

- defining the job to be done;
- defining the characteristics of the ideal candidate;
- attracting candidates;
- selecting candidates.

Before examining each in more detail, here is a word of warning. Many people think that the processes you are about to study are simple. After all, with large numbers of people unemployed, managers should have no difficulty in filling vacancies. If you talk to people currently involved in recruitment, they will probably tell you that their current difficulties lie, not in attracting candidates, but in choosing the most suitable from large numbers of applications.

In the 1930s, when the queues of unemployed people waited at factory gates for work, foremen would come and choose 'you, you and you'. Since then recruitment and selection techniques have developed in ways which help to give a better basis for decision-making. However, predictions about other people are subject to error. All recruiters make mistakes. Recruitment is more of an art than a science but systematically planned there should be less risk that you place 'square pegs in round holes'.

Stage 1. Defining the job to be done

Activity

Assume that someone is going to leave the department which you supervise. Draw a flow chart of the main decisions you would have to take in defining the job you want to be done by a replacement.

Your flow chart may have differed a little from figure 11. Compare the two and think about the reasons for any differences. In drawing the flow chart you might have been conscious of the need to link the early stages of recruitment and selection with the manpower planning process. When an employee leaves a job there is an opportunity to assess whether the job needs to be done at all or whether the work could usefully be reorganised.

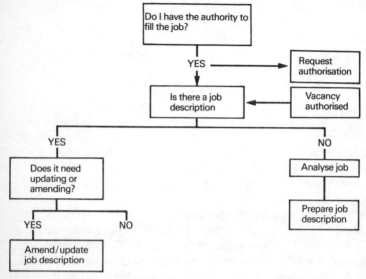

Figure 11. Defining the job to be done

Job analysis

The tasks which comprise the job must be analysed. This process
is known as job analysis. The main steps involved are:

- identifying the tasks involved in the job;
- examining how, when and why tasks are performed;
- identifying the main duties and responsibilities of the job;
- noting the physical, social and financial conditions of the job.

> *Self-check*
>
> Job analysis is a technique which generates basic informa-
> tion about the nature of tasks undertaken by employees. It
> can be used in many areas of personnel work. List five such
> areas.

ANSWER
- Appraisal (see Chapter 7).

- Training (see Chapter 8).
- Payment systems (see Chapter 12).
- Job evaluation (see Chapter 12).
- Disciplinary interviews (see Chapter 15).

Using job analysis you should be able to define the overall purpose or the role of the job in the organisation and the main tasks which the incumbent must carry out. It cannot be over-emphasised that an accurate job description is vital to the success of the rest of the recruitment and selection process. It is the basic building block on which advertising, interviewing and other processes are constructed.

Here is a job description for the post of assistant children's librarian.

Greenfields County Council

Libraries Department

Job title: Assistant Children's Librarian.
Responsible to: Assistant Librarian (Children's and Schools' Services).
Purpose: To assist in the effective provision by the Council of children's and schools' library services.

1 General duties

    1.1 Undertake such professional duties as may be required by the Assistant Librarian (children's and schools' services).

    1.2 Assist in the promotion of the use of the library service and reading with young people and parents.

    1.3 Participate in children's book selection and reviewing.

    1.4 Assist with the organisation of in-library activities as may be directed by senior children's and schools' library staff.

    1.5 Participate in the activities of the schools' library service.

    1.6 Undertake duties at any of the Council's libraries as directed by the Assistant Librarian (children's and schools' services).

2 Staff

    2.1 Control and supervise the work of non-professional staff in the absence of senior colleagues.

    2.2 Assist with the promotion of effective on-the-job training.

3 Resources

    3.1 Display a professional interest in current resources appropriate to the Childrens' Schools' Services and submit suggestions for additions to stock through the Senior Children's Librarian.

    3.2 Assist readers in the effective use of library resources.

4 Contacts

    4.1 Assistant Librarian Children's and Schools' Services, Senior Children's Librarian.

    4.2 Teachers.

    4.3 Playgroups and play scheme organisers and staff.

    4.4 Children and parents.

5 Work origin

    5.1 Children and parents.

    5.2 Teachers.

    5.3 Senior Children's and Schools' Services library staff.

    5.4 Play groups.

    5.5 Parents' associations and mothers' clubs.

    5.6 Other departments and groups interested in work with children.

6 Work disposal

    Same categories.

7 Circumstances

    The post holder will be located at the main library in the centre of Blanktown. There are also seven branch libraries in the surrounding district. The job holder will be required to work at these branch libraries from time to time.

Activity

Work through this job description. Try to decide whether it would give you all the information you need in order to begin the recruitment and selection process.

Some information is lacking. For example, though we are told that the job holder reports to the Assistant Librarian (Children's and Schools' Services) we do not know to whom this latter employee reports. In section 5.3 of the job description we are told that the tasks to be undertaken by the incumbent of this job may originate from 'Senior Children's and Schools' Services staff'. However, we do not know how these positions are related to the one described here. An organisation chart to show the staffing of the libraries would be helpful as a supporting document. In addition the 'circumstances' section is rather vague. What are the hours of work? What are the main features of the libraries service? Since the next stage of the process involves the development of a pen picture of the ideal candidate for the job, it would be useful to have an idea of the context of the job and of its non-material rewards.

Thus, the 'circumstances' section might continue as follows:

7.1 *Working conditions.* Old main library. Small offices. Post holder will share an office with the other Assistant Children's Librarian.

7.2 *Supervision received.* No close supervision. Main check is absence of complaints from originators of work.

7.3 *Consequences of error.* Receivers of service may be unaware of full range of services provided; delays in supply of books and teacher difficulties in schools may result.

7.4 *Difficulties.* Growing volume of work and enquiries. Pressure on schools' service in particular because of financial constraints on schools' ability to purchase new books.

7.5 *Satisfaction.* Interactions with children, young people and other users.

To be useful, job descriptions need to be full and accurate reflections of work done. A key task for personnel specialists and line managers is to ensure that job descriptions are regularly updated.

|| *Review*
|| List six features of an effective job description.

It should describe:

- the job;
- its place in the organisation;
- the circumstances under which it is performed;
- the objectives to be achieved by the job holder;

and it should be:

- a useful working document;
- up to date and relevant.

Stage 2. Defining the ideal candidate

Having prepared a job description for the vacancy under consideration, we now need to match the characteristics of the job with the characteristics of candidates who may apply for it. In order to undertake this process satisfactorily, we need a picture of the ideal candidate. Such a picture is called a 'person specification'.

Activity

Look back at the job description for the post of Assistant Children's Librarian (pp. 39–40) or at any other job description to which you have access. Try to list the main headings you would include when drawing up a person specification.

You may have listed a great many characteristics. A myriad of human attributes can be stipulated as requirements for the performance of jobs. It is usual to list the requirements under suitable headings. Below is the system most commonly used:

The 'seven point plan'*

1 Physical make-up – health, physique, appearance, hearing and speech.
2 Attainments – educational and occupational attainments and experience.
3 General intelligence – ability to reason quickly and accurately, to learn quickly and to handle complex ideas.
4 Specialised aptitudes – manual dexterity, mechanical aptitude, verbal or numerical facility, artistic aptitudes.
5 Interests – intellectual, practical and constructional, physically active, social and artistic.
6 Disposition – personality characteristics such as steadiness and self-reliance, acceptability to others, relationships with others.
7 Circumstances – domestic circumstances.

Whether you use this plan or another one, your aim will be to set a standard against which individual candidates can be matched. In doing this you may recognise the difficulty of attracting a candidate who is ideal on *all* the attributes listed.

*Professor Alec Rodger, *The Seven Point Plan*, National Institute of Industrial Psychology, 1952

Self-check

Why is this? How can you write a person specification to take account of this difficulty of finding the ideal candidate?

Even in times of high unemployment, there are still shortages. For example, at present many companies find it difficult to recruit experienced computer staff. It is usual to distinguish between those features of the candidate which are absolutely essential and those which are desirable. For example, if you used the 'seven point plan' as the framework for a person specification for the post of Assistant Children's Librarian, you might write:

Attainments
Essential
Chartered Librarian with two years' post-qualification experience.

Desirable
As above plus one year's experience in children's and/or schools' library service.

In writing person specifications, it is important to try to be as precise as if you were writing a specification for a piece of machinery.

Stage 3. Attracting candidates

Having written a person specification, it is necessary to encourage some people to become applicants.

Self-check

List three possible sources of applicants for jobs.

ANSWER

- Internal advertisements or analysis of personnel records.
- External advertisements.
- Employment agencies – private or public.

Your list also might have included:

- Schools, colleges or other institutions providing training courses.

- Casual callers or writers of letters.
- Recommendations from existing employees.

Advertisements

Over 4,000 publications in the UK carry recruitment advertisements. As well as the written word, employers use radio, television and computerised information systems such as Oracle and Prestel. Here we are concerned with the principles of effective recruitment advertising. These can be established by answering the following questions.

Where am I likely to find potential candidates? You need to know where candidates are likely to be currently working or undergoing education or training and where they live. Some candidates will be found in the local labour market, because their skills can be used by many employers; those who occupy specialist positions are part of a national labour market. There would be little point in a local solicitor advertising for a typist in a national newspaper!

How can I attract them to work for me? A useful way to answer this is to put yourself in the candidate's shoes. What would be the attractions of this particular job?

> *Activity*
>
> You are a sixteen-year-old school leaver thinking of applying for a job in a supermarket as a check-out operator. List the details you would require before applying for the job.

I divided my list into two parts:

Vital information
- Earnings (including any bonus).
- Perks, e.g. discount on goods, overalls, canteen, other staff facilities.
- Hours of work.
- Holidays.

Other information
- Company name, size, location, etc.
- Conditions of work, rush hours, quiet times.
- Training.
- Promotion prospects.
- Job security.
- Notice periods.

Your list may differ to some degree from this one. The general point is that designing a recruitment advertisement is a marketing exercise in which the preferences of potential candidates should be compared with the features of the job (taken from the job description). Those aspects which are most likely to appeal can be emphasised.

If there are significant problems in recruiting candidates who equate to the requirements of the personnel specification, you may wish to consider the specific advantages and disadvantages of the job to identify the selling points.

Activity

Go to your local supermarket. Talk to a teenage check-out operator about the attractions of this job.

The teenager with whom I spoke said: 'I like always meeting people and there are quite a few people of my own age working here so there is a nice atmosphere.' I could amend the personnel specification for this job to take account of these comments if I felt that these views would be widely shared by other workers. In any case it is useful if a recruitment advertisement contains a brief profile of the ideal applicant.

There are no prizes for writing advertisements which attract the largest possible number of candidates. The aim should be to recruit the right quality of candidates. If the characteristics of the ideal candidate are succinctly expressed, then only suitable candidates are likely to apply. With three million people unemployed this is often wishful thinking! However, it should cut out some of the wasted effort involved in responding to a vast number of applicants, most of whom are unsuitable or marginal.

Review activity

Analyse the content of advertisements for jobs in the current edition of your local newspaper. List five attributes of an effective advertisement.

ANSWER

- A compelling headline.
- Interesting content.
- Clear, unambiguous information about the job and the likely candidate.
- Information on how to apply.
- Eye-catching design and typography.

External recruitment agencies

Several options are open to organisations which choose to use an external agency for recruitment purposes:

- government agencies – in UK, the Job Centre or Professional and Executive Register (PER);
- private employment agencies;
- selection consultants to provide a shortlist of candidates;
- executive search consultants or 'head-hunters', who will contact suitable candidates direct;
- advertising agencies to design and place advertisements;
- some combination of these.

Some of these options can be expensive. Selection consultants can charge up to 20 per cent of the annual salary of the job to be filled. However, those who use them often argue that they are cost-effective.

Review

List six factors which influence the choice of a recruitment channel or source of applicants.

ANSWER

- Past experience.

- The audience to be reached.
- The nature of the job.
- The desired image of the employing organisation.
- Cost-effectiveness.
- Time required to fill the vacancy.

Stage 4. Selecting candidates

Looking forward – self-check

Draw a flowchart of the main stages of the selection process from receiving applications to making an appointment.

How similar is your flowchart to figure 12? Variations are possible depending on the requirements of the organisation. For example, medical examinations may be used for older applicants, where jobs are particularly physically demanding and where safety is vital (e.g. airline pilots). In other cases medical history questionnaires are often sufficient. A further area of difference may be that of references. The important point to gain from the exercise lies in the design of a systematic assessment process.

Self-check

What objective is the employer trying to achieve in the selection process?

ANSWER

- To get the right person for the job.
- To establish or maintain an image as a good employer.
- To make the process as cost-effective as possible.

As in advertising, there is a need to encourage an element of self-selection by potential candidates. Many employers send applicants further information about the organisation, the job and the ideal candidate. Some applicants may withdraw after matching their characteristics against the requirements of the job. Whether the provision of such information is appropriate depends on the nature of the job.

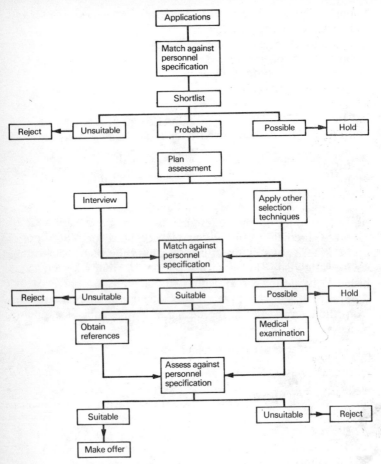

Figure 12. Flowchart of the selection process

Shortlisting

For many jobs it is possible to eliminate the majority of candidates without even seeing them. Letters of application, *curricula vitae* and, above all, application forms can be used as screening devices. Letters of application and *c.v.*s are less likely to be vague if the advertisement is specific about the nature of the job and the person required to perform it; nevertheless, there are usually more problems in matching information thus received from applicants than if it is presented on a well-designed application form.

By now you should be used to the notion that recruitment and selection techniques should be designed with an eye to the nature of the job and of the organisation. An application form is no different. For reasons of cost and simplicity most personnel practitioners find it adequate to use four or so basic types of form – for graduate entrants, manual workers, routine non-manual jobs, and professional and managerial occupations.

> *Activity*
>
> Look again at the job advertisements in your local newspaper. Telephone three organisations for application forms. List three types of information which all the forms require.

- Personal details – name, address, date of birth, etc.;
- education;
- job history or work experience.

Other details will be required depending on the type of job and organisation. For more responsible jobs it is quite common to require candidates to write a general statement about their suitability for the job.

Interviewing

Research shows that selection by this method can be no more reliable than sticking pins in a list of names. Nor is it a valid selection method. Validity is concerned with how well the assessment procedure predicts future successful job performance; reliability is the degree to which the same or a different interviewer would reach the same selection decision. We would have little confidence in a thermometer which gave different readings in boiling water on different days! If something is not reliable, it cannot be valid. However, survey data indicates that almost all organisations use the interview as a means of selection.

> *Self-check*
>
> Re-read the general objectives of selection processes (see p. 47). If interviews are neither a valid nor a reliable means of selecting candidates, why do most employers use them?

Your answer may have been simply that many interviewers don't recognise the problems described above. You may have also included some of the following points:

- Interviewing may be cheaper than other selection methods, especially tests.
- The interview allows candidates to obtain information about the job and the organisation as well as providing a medium within which they may be judged by the interviewer.
- After any interview candidates should feel that they have had a fair deal from the organisation.
- If the interview is conducted by the person to whom the new employee would report, it allows the parties to assess their mutual compatibility.

Whatever the interview's validity or reliability, most employers will continue to use it. Probably the best way is to use trained interviewers, who are aware of the problems inherent in the technique. Some of these problems are summarised in figure 13.

The halo effect and interview bias

If you ever have to interview someone with the same educational or work background as yourself, beware of the halo effect! You may assume that, because the candidate shares some aspect of your background or your interests, he must share your characteristics as a bright, successful human being! Or must he? It is rumoured that junior doctors in teaching hospitals often are selected more for their prowess at rugby than for their medical skills. The 'old boy network' operates similarly – one of the reasons why women find it difficult to break into the echelons of power.

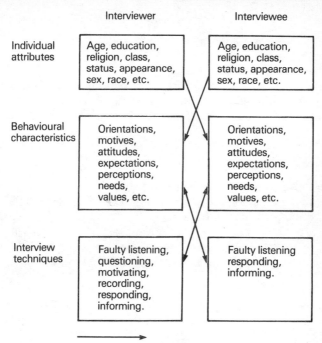

Presumed direction of influence

Figure 13. The behavioural characteristics of the interview

Interviewer bias sometimes may be based on physical characteristics. Some people dislike people with beards or long hair.

Both the halo effect and bias make it likely that the interviewer decides for or against the candidate in the first few minutes of the interview. The rest of the time is then spent trying to prove first impressions accurate. Listening, questioning, motivating, recording and so on are likely to be geared to this end.

Self check looking forward

From your experiences as an interviewee and from our discussion so far, what do you think can be done to combat these problems inherent in the selection interview?

ANSWER

- Systematic preparation.
- The interviewer should try to be aware of the nature of his own prejudices, both negative and positive.
- Concentrate on the advantages of the interview – assessing compatibility, giving information about the job, etc.
- Train interviewers.

Systematic preparation

Interviewers must be well informed about both the job description and the personnel specification. They should brief themselves adequately about the candidate. A well-designed application form is vital here. Preparation should go beyond being able to read the candidate's own words back to him from the application form! This is likely to frustrate applicants.

Questioning techniques

'Effective interviewers ask good questions.' This is one of the most important interviewing skills.

Open questions One of the key purposes of selection interviewing is to elicit information to enable the candidate's characteristics to be matched against the personnel specification:

- 'Why did you apply for this job?'
- 'Why did you choose that course?'

Closed questions These are questions to which the only answer can be 'Yes', 'No' or 'I don't know'. They may be used to check information or to get a definite response quickly. An interview which relies heavily on these is rather wooden. Such questions may push the candidate into false polarisations. For example, the question, 'Did you enjoy your college course?', may provoke the answer, 'Yes', where the reality could be much more complex. More garrulous or helpful candidates may expand the answer without prompting, but the interviewer should be aware that he is relinquishing control over the interview.

Probing questions Sometimes the candidate's answers will lack depth or clarity: 'I left that job because I felt the career prospects were non-existent.' The interviewer probably needs to know the reasons why the candidate felt this. He can probe by asking: 'Why do you say that?' . . . 'What kind of career development did you want?' Sometimes the response to such a question will be slow. The time taken to reply probably indicates that it is an effective probing question.

Multiple questions If the interviewer had asked both my probing questions at the same time, he would have been using a multiple question. These are faulty since the candidate can choose which question to answer. Again the interviewer is in danger of surrendering control of the situation.

Linking questions or statements An interview should be a conversation with a purpose. One useful way of achieving this is for the interviewer to indicate, that a particular area of questioning is complete, and that it is time to look at another topic: 'Now that we've discussed your work experience, can we have a look at your activities outside work?'

Leading questions These should be avoided in selection interviews since they are likely to feed the interviewer's own prejudices and desire to confirm early impressions: 'We are anxious to appoint someone who is good at dealing with the public. You'd be all right there, wouldn't you?' What fool is going to deny this?

Problem-centred questions You may wish to get some impression about the response of the candidate to particular situations: 'Could you tell me about the most difficult customer you had to deal with when you were doing that Saturday job?' Such questions are very useful provided that they are relevant to the job in question and can be answered realistically by the interviewee.

Indirect questions If you ask a candidate, 'Do you get on with other people?' you are passing control of the interview to the interviewee. It is probably better to get the candidate to describe relationships with fellow workers or friends or how he has behaved in particular situations. Then you can judge how successfully he interacts with other people.

Review

Below is a list of questions which might be asked in a selection interview. What kind of question is each one? Could they be rephrased in any way for greater effectiveness?

1 'Did you leave school in 1969?'
2 'Did you get your professional qualification in 1973 and then decide that it was time to get a better job?'
3 'What made you decide to become an architect?'
4 'You said that you disliked your first job. Why was that?'
5 'I see that you spent three years working in West Africa. That'd be long enough for anyone, wouldn't you say?'
6 'What would you do if your spaceship crash-landed on the moon?'
7 'How good are you at making difficult decisions?'

ANSWERS

1 A closed question. It does not yield much information and may be irritating to the candidate, if the information is included on the application form.
2 A multiple question. The answer to the first part could be on the application form. The second part is a leading question. The questioner seems to be assuming that the job which he then took was a better job, or that the acquisition of a qualification prompted the change of job. It might be more effective to ask, 'Why did you change your job in 1973?' If reasons other than qualifications, are given, the next question could be, 'How did you feel when you became professionally qualified?'
3 A very open question. The answer is likely to need probing.
4 A probing question. The information that the candidate did not like a particular job would be too vague to be helpful in any judgement about suitability for a job.
5 A leading question. Is the interviewer revealing any bias? It could be reworded, 'Why did you spend three years working in West Africa?'

6 A problem-centred question. You should be critical of its relevance, unless you assume that it was used to interview astronauts!

7 A direct and fairly meaningless question. If you are looking for a decisive individual, it is probably better to ask indirect questions. For example, the candidate could be asked to describe a difficult situation recently encountered at work.

Stress interviews

These attempt to simulate the stress generated by the job situation in order to assess whether the candidate would be able to cope. Some interviews for managerial positions are structured in this way. The problems of validity and reliability discussed earlier lead me to be sceptical about this approach. Indeed, with some candidates, they may be counter-productive. A friend of mine was shown into an office for an interview. Behind a desk sat a man obscured from sight by the newspaper he was reading. My friend waited. Presumably there was an attempt to create stress by the ambiguity of the situation. My friend was immensely irritated and left. Would he have been suitable for the job? Could an interviewer make an accurate judgement from his reaction to this situation? I doubt it!

Interview structure

To establish rapport early in the interview, it is useful to start the questioning in the candidate's 'home territory', for example, asking for a description of the most recent job. Many experienced interviewers say that they have difficulty in ensuring that they always cover all the relevant ground during an interview. A checklist based, for example, on the headings of the 'seven point plan' or of the personnel specification is helpful. This may then form a basis for the interview structure. Details about the job can be given after obtaining information about the candidate. This obviates the necessity of giving this to obviously unsuitable candidates. Time should be allowed for questions from the candidate.

Panel interviews

In the public sector in the UK it is common to use panel interviews, where a candidate faces several interviewers at once. Opinions differ as to whether these are more or less valid than one-to-one interviews. Broadly, the following principles should be observed for panel interviews:

- All participants should have a genuine claim to be involved.
- All interviewers should be skilled and experienced.
- Proper planning and coordination are vital.
- It is probably better to use a 'tight' structure, where each interviewer takes a particular role and a chairman acts as coordinator.

Activity

Talk to a number of practised interviewers about their experiences of interviewing. Or talk to friends or colleagues about their experiences as interviewees. Compile a list of ten items headed 'The dont's of interviewing'.

Interviewers should not:

- keep the interviewee waiting;
- interview without systematic preparation and planning;
- allow the interview to be interrupted;
- ask trick questions, leading questions, multiple questions or too many closed questions;
- lose control of the interview to the interviewee;
- fail to give the candidate information about the job;
- take copious notes during the interview;
- display bias or prejudice;
- talk too much (probably not more than one third of the interview time);
- allow the candidate to gloss over important points.

This list is not exhaustive and some of the points overlap. Think about the differences between your list and mine.

Selection testing

Selection tests are used to provide a standardised, reliable, objective measure of applicants' skills. There are two main types:

- tests of capacity;
- tests of personality and attitudes.

Tests of capacity

Some jobs require the use of specialist skills. For example, aptitude tests have been devised to test the capacity of potential computer programmers. Other tests of capacity may be more general. For example, many tests are concerned with mental ability. Postmen are tested for literacy, powers of observation, speed in perception and checking information, short-term memory and the ability to translate a code into comprehensible instructions. Another well-known group of tests aims to measure general mental ability or intelligence. This can be defined as the ability to learn and to use learning to reason. Such tests are often used for graduate entrants. Manual dexterity tests are used in the clothing industry to test how quickly and accurately a simple assembly task can be carried out.

Tests of personality and attitude

These fall into two categories:

- questionnaires (usually multiple-choice, paper-and-pencil tests);
- projective techniques (where the candidate is asked to project himself into the test situation).

The most famous of this latter group is probably the Rorschach ink blot test used in psychology, though it is not commonly used in personnel selection. One of the most popular questionnaires is the 16PF personality test, which yields scores on sixteen personality factors.

This is a very brief description of the variety of tests available for selection purposes. If you ever consider using tests you should be aware of the range of specialist services available.

Validation of tests

Tests should have been validated for use with particular occupational groups. In other words it should have been possible to show that high performers on the test are the most successful in job performance and vice versa for low test performers. Surveys suggest that significant numbers of employers do not attempt to validate the tests they use; however, tests *must* be validated for three reasons:

- to ensure that they are able to predict job success;
- to show how fairly the test samples the candidate's knowledge or skill;
- to assess how far the test can measure what it purports to measure. (For example, tests of leadership should be capable of measuring leadership traits and leadership should be vital to effective job performance.)

Recently concern has been expressed that selection tests may be biased against minority groups. This area is examined in Chapter 6.

Self-check

List four situations in which it might be advantageous to use selection tests.

ANSWER

- When large numbers of people must be recruited.
- When as a consequence of the numbers involved the use of tests would be cost-effective.
- When it is impossible to rely on educational qualifications as a predictor of job success.
- When sufficient time is available to validate the tests on the particular occupational group for which the test has been designed.

References

|| *Looking forward – self-check*
|| Give two reasons for the use of references in selection.

ANSWER

- To supplement information elicited by the use of other selection methods.
- To check the veracity of the candidate's statements.

In practice this area is fraught with problems. Applicants are unlikely to name referees who will indicate their unsuitability for a job. Some people suggest for this reason that references from a previous employer, who is less likely to gloss over the problem areas, should be used. Will this always be so? Probably not. Some employers will simply lack awareness of the job. The more unscrupulous may deliberately mislead, by writing either a glowing reference about an employee they wish to lose or an unfavourable one about an employee they wish to retain.

|| *Self-check*
|| List three ways in which references may be made more
|| reliable.

ANSWER

- Ask a previous employer for factual information only (dates of employment, job title, reason for leaving, etc.).
- Check doubtful information by telephone.
- Provide a structure or short questionnaire for the referee to follow.

The follow-up process

Once the candidate has started work, those involved in recruitment and selection are tempted to heave a sigh of relief and turn to other problems. This is unwise. Two types of follow-up system should be designed:

- individual follow-up or induction (see Chapter 4);

- evaluation of the recruitment and selection process to ensure that mistakes are avoided in future.

Evaluation procedures

Looking forward – self-check

Why is it necessary to have information about the effectiveness of the recruitment and selection process? Give three reasons.

ANSWER

- To seek improvements in policies and procedures.
- To calculate costs. Recruitment and selection are an expensive part of personnel management practice.
- To provide feedback into manpower planning. For example, it may be very difficult to fill certain jobs; this will require questions to be answered about the nature of the jobs and of the people required to perform them.

Rigorous evaluation of the effectiveness of procedures will provide useful information. However, it must be emphasised that this is a difficult exercise. An example will indicate some possible reasons for this. If a company recruits graduates and a large proportion leave within a year, where does the fault lie? In the recruitment and selection process? In the training programme? In the nature of the tasks they are required to perform? In the salaries paid? Or may the reason be demand for their skills elsewhere in the labour market? Evaluation will need to be in depth rather than a superficial analysis only of recruitment and selection procedures and practices.

Self-check

By what means can an organisation judge the effectiveness of its recruitment and selection procedures?

On p. 37 at the beginning of this chapter, we defined the recruitment and selection process as consisting of four stages:

- defining the job to be done;
- defining the characteristics of the ideal candidate;
- attracting candidates;
- selecting candidates.

Procedures need to be designed to evaluate each stage.

> *Activity*
>
> Think of one question to ask to evaluate each stage of the recruitment and selection process.

ANSWER

Stage 1 Is the job description an accurate representation of the tasks which the job holder performs?

Stage 2 Is it possible to recruit candidates who match the personnel specification's description of the ideal candidate?

Stage 3 What is the cost of recruitment advertising as a proportion of the annual payroll? (Costs in different years and in the same year in different departments will be useful.)

Stage 4 How do assessors' judgements at the time of selection compare with candidates' actual performance in the job?

Evaluation of recruitment and selection by obtaining the answers to such questions is a very useful way to get a 'feel' for the validity of the whole process.

Managerial roles in recruitment and selection

In Chapter 1 we discussed the respective roles of personnel practitioners and other members of management in personnel management.

> *Review*
>
> List five terms which we used there to describe the role of personnel specialists in the management of people at work.

ANSWER

- Audit.
- Executive.
- Facilitator.
- Consultancy.
- Service.

> *Activity*
>
> Recruitment and selection activities of personnel special-
> ists can be described in terms of the five general roles listed
> above. Give an example from this area of personnel
> management for each of the five terms listed above.

ANSWERS

Audit Checking to establish that job descriptions supplied by
managers reflect the true nature of the tasks.

Executive Placing advertisements in the local or the national
press.

Facilitator Ensuring that line managers and others involved in
recruitment and selection have the necessary knowledge and
skills to play their part in this activity effectively.

Consultancy Advice to managers on selection decisions.

Service Providing managers with response rate data on recruitment advertising to enable joint decisions to be made on the most
effective way to attract a pool of applicants.

4 | Introducing the individual to the organisation

In this chapter we focus on the new employee's early 'life' with the organisation. This process of entry to jobs is commonly termed 'induction'. By the end of this chapter you should be familiar with the methods of helping employees to cope with a new job in a strange organisation. However, it is also important that you understand the reasons for giving attention to this stage of employment.

Studies have shown that where attention is given to induction the rate of labour turnover among new employees is lower. The existence of what has been termed the 'induction crisis' gives us a rationale for the development of techniques which aim generally to ease the entry of the individual into the organisation.

Review

Remembering the work which we did in Chapter 2, sketch the curve which depicts the process of labour turnover. Your curve should include the initial peak or induction crisis (see Chapter 2, p. 19).

Activity

Go and talk to anyone who supervises or manages staff. Explain the process of labour turnover to them. Discuss the possibility of reducing or eliminating the effects of the induction crisis. After your discussion list three ways of possibly achieving this. Do you think it would be a good idea to eliminate it altogether?

Ways of reducing the effects of the induction crisis

- Get better information about candidates during recruitment and selection. This should improve selection decisions.

- Give candidates better information about the job on offer. To some degree people select themselves for jobs. This may include information which will cause candidates to withdraw or to refuse an offer of employment, should one be forthcoming. Some advertisements for social workers, for example, say: 'Want to be run off your feet, overworked, under-appreciated? . . . Then join our busy team.' In this way new recruits at least know what to expect.
- Improve the induction process. (This is covered later in this chapter.)

Should the induction crisis be eliminated?

Many organisations which are resourceful in 'tying people to the organisation with golden chains', such as low-cost mortgages or non-contributory pension schemes, then regret the absence of turnover. Labour turnover does have positive aspects for the organisation.

Self-check

What do you see as the benefits of labour turnover?

- Allows new blood into the organisation.
- Eliminates 'dead wood'.
- Creates opportunities for promotion.
- Reduces labour costs. Often employees who leave are near the top of the salary scale; new appointees start lower down.
- Creates flexibility for restructuring of work.

Review

List three aims of the induction process.

ANSWER

- To make the new employee efficient as quickly as possible.
- To encourage the new employee to become committed to the organisation and thus less likely to leave quickly.
- To familiarise the new employee with the job so that the feeling of being 'out of place' is quickly dispelled.

The induction process

Those who have worked in organisations for some time forget what it felt like to be new. They take for granted their ways of working, the language they use at work and the accepted ways of dealing with colleagues, superiors, subordinates and clients. Departments, committees and other working groups are frequently referred to by initials.

Recently I have been involved in an organisation with an 'IR' group. My own background led me to believe that this was an 'industrial relations group'. I was wrong! 'IR' in this case stood for 'information retrieval' – very confusing to the newcomer! Another example of the 'taken-for-granted' nature of organisational life comes from some research I did in the hairdressing industry. A new apprentice in a high-class salon was asked by a stylist to buy some sandwiches for an important client from a neighbouring snack bar. She returned with them in a paper bag and gave them to the client not realising that this was unacceptable behaviour. Someone who 'knew the ropes' would have transferred the sandwiches to a plate before delivering them! Her embarrassment at this and other incidents led her to seek other employment.

From such stories as these you should realise the importance of giving attention to the induction process. New employees usually want to do a 'fair day's work for a fair day's pay'. They want to be accepted by their colleagues and to feel generally comfortable in the organisation and in their job. Management wants workers who will quickly become efficient and committed. The aim of the induction process is to meet the needs of both parties in a mutually acceptable way.

Though this aim is probably universally applicable, induction programmes must be designed to fit the characteristics of the job and of its organisational context. For example very small companies are unlikely to organise formal induction courses or to give employees printed handbooks. Nevertheless, attention should be given to the types of information required by the new employee.

Activity

Happy Days is a large group of catering companies with hotels, restaurants and motorway service stations all over Britain. Brown's Hotel situated in central London is one of the group's largest establishments. You are a receptionist at Brown's Hotel. It is your first day. List five questions which you would want to ask today as part of the process of becoming familiar with your job and the company for which you work.

Your five items should be contained in the following list:

- To whom do I give my income tax form, birth certificate, work permit, or any other information which my new employer requires?
- Do I have to sign in when I arrive for work each day, and if so, where?
- From whom do I collect my pay and when?
- Where do I eat my lunch and at what time?
- Do I get a coffee or tea break? When? Who relieves me?
- Where are the toilets and washing facilities?
- Whom do I need to meet to do my job effectively – my boss, heads of departments in the hotel, etc.?
- Where do I go or whom do I ask for help, if I cannot answer telephone or other queries?
- How do I operate the hotel switchboard, the typewriter and any other equipment necessary for me to perform my job efficiently?

Compare your questions with mine. I expect that there are some differences. Much depends on the information given to the potential employee during selection and the new employee's general familiarity with similar work.

To summarise, on the first day it is necessary to ensure that new employees:

- do not feel lost or foolish;
- do not endanger themselves or other people because they are not given vital safety information.

Provided that this is done, there are no other hard-and-fast rules about this stage of the induction process. It is generally unwise to communicate a great deal of information orally to new employees at this time. The stress of the first day in a new environment can be equated with 'culture shock'. The danger is that little will be remembered. It is wise to provide written 'back-up' to vital information communicated orally for this reason. An employee handbook is useful here.

Activity

What information should be included in an employee handbook? (Look at the one used in your own organisation if you can.) List five items.

Again I have included more than five items in my list:

- Brief description of the organisation – numbers employed, locations, products, etc.
- Basic conditions of employment – pay scales, holidays, pension arrangements, hours of work.
- Sickness arrangements – notification, pay, certification.
- Disciplinary and grievance procedures.
- Trade union membership and collective bargaining arrangements.
- Staff purchase arrangements and other 'perks'.
- Travelling and subsistence arrangements.
- Medical and welfare facilities.
- Canteen facilities.
- Health and safety arrangements.
- Education and training policies and facilities.

This list is by no means exhaustive. The content of employee handbooks varies depending on such organisational characteristics as numbers employed, jobs performed and managerial policies and practices. Handbooks need not be glossy and should be written clearly and concisely with the information needs of the employee as the focus.

Induction training

Many organisations run induction courses as a formal mechanism for the induction of new employees.

> *Self-check*
>
> What three factors would the personnel manager of Brown's Hotel have to take into account in deciding whether or not it would be useful to design a formal induction training course?

ANSWER

- The numbers of new employees likely to enter the hotel in the foreseeable future for whom a formal induction training programme would be necessary.
- The minimum viable group size for such a course.
- The maximum period of employment before which a formal induction training programme would become superfluous.

Content and timing of induction training courses

If it is decided that such a course might be beneficial to some or all new employees, careful attention must be given to content and timing. A good starting point is what does the new entrant want to know and when? The answer is that the needs of new entrants differ considerably. For example, new members of management probably require more detailed information about organisation structure, policies and practices than will more junior clerical staff or manual workers. There are probably disadvantages in arranging for new employees to attend off-the-job induction courses too early. Initially it is likely that they will be keen to familiarise themselves with the immediate requirements of the job which they are to perform. However, in a relatively short time they should be ready to know more about the organisation in which they work.

Self-check

List six elements which should be included in a one-day induction programme for employees of Brown's Hotel.

ANSWER

- The structure of the Happy Days Group and of Brown's Hotel.
- Tour of the hotel.
- Payment systems including sick pay and holiday arrangements.
- Company employment policies.
- Training and promotion practices and opportunities.
- Open forum. (Any questions?)

Having sketched out a design for an induction programme, it will be necessary to ensure that it fits the needs of new employees. One way of doing this is to run one or more 'pilot' courses which are carefully evaluated by both trainees and others with a direct interest in the area. (For further information on methods of evaluating training programmes see Chapter 8.)

Attention should also be given to the training methods utilised to convey information to new employees.

Self-check

It is possible to convey information about organisation structures and products to members of an induction training course by a number of different methods. List four of these.

ANSWER

- Film or videotape.
- Tape/slide presentation.
- Written handout supplemented by question and answer session.
- Lecture.

Departmental induction

A more informal induction process is probably just as important as a training course. For the new employee it may be far more important, at least in the initial stages of employment with an organisation, to get to know one's colleagues and the nature of one's job, than to be given more general information about the employing organisation. In a large organisation it is likely that the personnel or training department will carry responsibility for the formal part of the induction process, but line managers and supervisors should not abdicate responsibility for the less formal process. New employees should at least be welcomed by their departmental manager even if – as commonly occurs – the immediate supervisor is mainly responsible for introducing the new employee to the job and to workmates. In small companies where it would not be economic to organise a formal induction course, it is even more vital that someone (probably the supervisor) is responsible for introducing each new employee to the organisation. A checklist of items to be covered would be a useful aid to ensure this is carried out effectively.

Review

Line managers, supervisors, fellow workers, personnel and training staff all have a role to play in the induction of new workers. List one activity which may be carried out by each of these to assist in the process.

ANSWERS

Departmental managers
●Welcoming new employees to the department.

Supervisors
●Explaining the job to the new employee and providing support in the early days.

Fellow workers
●Making the new employee feel welcome and comfortable in the work group.

Personnel staff
●Explaining conditions of employment very early in the employment of the newcomer.

Training staff
●Designing induction courses or other training aids relevant to the needs of new employees.

A final word

Throughout this chapter we have stressed the need to design induction procedures with the perspective and needs of the new employee in mind. To ensure that this has been achieved it will be useful to review systematically the experiences of newcomers and other relevant employees (for example, supervisors, training and personnel specialists) in order that unsatisfactory elements can be changed. Many organisations do not do this; there is a plethora of film and video material about organisations which is either too remote from the newcomer's likely experience or so facile that it leads only to mockery! New employees might be prepared to voice such criticisms if only they were asked to speak!

5 | The law and the rights of the new employee

In order to be able to work within the law so far as employment is concerned you must understand the basic framework of the English legal system. Therefore we begin this chapter with an examination of the legal framework of employee rights in the UK. This is also a vital 'building block' for the work that you will do in Chapters 11 and 15. The rest of this chapter focuses on the ways in which the law influences the rights of the new employee. We shall examine relevant areas of the law on race and sex discrimination, the rights of trade unionists, the disabled and those who have been convicted of crimes. This is followed by a discussion of the rights and obligations of employers and employees when there is a contract of employment between them.

The legal framework of employees' rights

Employment law contains provisions relating both to collective bargaining, or the rights of employees as trade unionists, and to the rights at work of individual employees. In this book we are concerned mainly with the latter area. The collective rights of employees in law are dealt with in *Understanding Industrial Relations* by Chris Brewster, Pan Breakthrough Books, 1984.

Employees' legal rights are not only created by Acts of Parliament or statutes. They come also from case law. The English legal system can be distinguished from that of most other countries by the extent to which judges and tribunals are bound to follow the decisions of judges in higher courts unless they feel that the facts of the previous cases were substantially different. For this reason such judgements are called case law. Thus, in making decisions, members of tribunals and judges are bound by decisions made in higher courts; this is known as 'judicial precedent'.

In the area of employment law, it is normally sufficient for managers to be aware of the main *statutory* provisions. This book can merely scratch the surface in this area; it is not intended to turn you into a lawyer. You should be aware of the limits of your knowledge if you are called on to make decisions which might affect employees' legal rights, and should be prepared to ask for specialist advice.

Activity

Talk to anyone who supervises or manages workers. Ask them where they would go for advice on employment law. After your discussion list three sources of help.

ANSWER

- The Advisory, Conciliation and Arbitration Service (ACAS).
- The organisation's personnel department.
- A regularly updated employment law case book.

They might also have mentioned an employers' association. Not all firms belong to such associations, however. (For the functions of employers' associations, see Chapter 2 of *Understanding Industrial Relations* by Chris Brewster, Pan Breakthrough Books, 1984.) Private consultants may also be used.

The role of ACAS in individual rights legislation

The Advisory, Conciliation and Arbitration Service automatically receives copies of all individual legal claims to tribunals except those which are concerned only with redundancy compensation. Normally employees must make claims within three months of the occurrence of the event which forms the basis of their complaint. ACAS has specialist conciliation officers to assist in employment law cases. Often this official contacts the parties or their representatives and tries to help them reach a settlement before the case goes to a tribunal. He will often do this by suggesting, from experience, the likely outcome if the case goes to a tribunal. About half the cases raised by employees result in a settlement at this stage.

Industrial tribunals

If conciliation fails, the case will go to a tribunal. Tribunals, which are organised on a regional basis, consist of a legally qualified chairman and two 'side members', representing the two sides – employers and employees – of industry. These are selected from a panel drawn up by the Secretary of State for Employment from nominations from the Trades Union Congress, the Confederation of British Industry, the Department of Employment and other bodies. In practice nominees often have trade union, personnel management or other relevant work experience.

Tribunal procedure is relatively informal. Employees are often represented by trade union officials and employers sometimes use legal representatives. Tribunal decisions do not set precedents in making decisions. Tribunals are bound by decisions of higher courts but not of other industrial tribunals. They do not normally award 'costs' in favour of the winning party, though they may do so where one party has acted 'frivolously or vexatiously'.

Appeals against tribunal decisions

If there is an appeal on a point of law against the tribunal's decision, the case will go to the Employment Appeal Tribunal (EAT) and thence to the Court of Appeal and ultimately to the House of Lords. Whilst these latter courts are part of the mainstream of the English legal system, the EAT was established in 1975 specifically to deal with appeals from industrial tribunals and other aspects of labour law. As compared with other courts of law, its procedures are relatively informal, but it has all the powers of the High Court. On each case heard, there will be a judge and normally two lay members drawn from a panel of people with specialist knowledge of industrial relations.

Review

Draw a flowchart to illustrate the progress of an individual's claim against an employer for unfair dismissal or race or sex discrimination from its inception to a hearing in the Employment Appeal Tribunal (EAT).

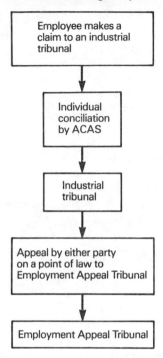

Figure 14. The progress of an employment law case from inception to a hearing by the Employment Appeal Tribunal

The law and the rights of job applicants

Job applicants are protected from discrimination by employers on grounds of:

- sex;
- maritial status;
- colour;
- race;
- nationality;
- ethnic or national origin.

The main statutes here are the Sex Discrimination Act 1975 and the Race Relations Act 1976.

Other groups protected by law to some degree as job applicants are the disabled and those who have been convicted of offences in court. The relevant statutes here are the Disabled Persons (Employment) Acts 1944 and 1958 and the Rehabilitation of Offenders Act 1974.

What is discrimination?

Both the Sex Discrimination Act and the Race Relations Act define three kinds of discrimination.

1 Direct discrimination Suppose you saw a noticeboard like this advertising vacancies outside a factory:

> BLOGGS ENGINEERING LIMITED
> VACANCIES
>
> JOINER
> HGV CLASS 1 DRIVER
> UNIVERSAL MILLER
>
> BLACKS AND WOMEN NEED NOT APPLY

You would probably be very surprised, since such overtly discriminatory behaviour tends to be unacceptable today. Indeed, such a notice is illegal in that it indicates that Bloggs Engineering Limited intends to treat black and female applicants for jobs less favourably than other people. This is direct discrimination.

2 Indirect discrimination

> WANTED HOSPITAL PORTERS
>
> Applicants must be able to pass an
> English language test and lift very
> heavy objects
>
> ST FLORENCE'S HOSPITAL

How would this advertisement fare under the anti-discrimination legislation? It could be argued that it is indirect discrimination; that is, the job requirements specified may favour one sex or racial group more than another. This would be the case if:

- the proportion of people of a particular racial group or sex, who could comply with the job requirements specified, was considerably smaller than the proportion of people outside those groups; *and*
- St Florence's Hospital could not justify the conditions.

In this example the hospital would need to demonstrate that it was necessary and not merely convenient for porters to speak English to the standard required by the test. Previous cases have shown that employers cannot automatically justify on health and safety grounds the non-selection of applicants who speak poor English. Of course, staff must be able to understand safety instructions and safety notices, but is the testing of applicants' proficiency in English the *only* way of ensuring that the requirements of the Health and Safety at Work Act are met?

Self-check

How else could St Florence's ensure that their porters could understand safety instructions and safety notices?

There are several possible solutions. One way would be to translate safety notices and other information into relevant languages. For illiterate new employees it might be possible to use clearly understood symbols. Another alternative would be to provide safety training in the relevant languages. A further possibility would be to offer English language training.

Is it also indirect discrimination, this time against women, to require applicants to lift heavy weights? This would depend on whether it could be proved that fewer women than men could meet the test of strength laid down by the hospital for entry to the job. If this was the case, then St Florence's would have to demonstrate that the nature of a porter's job required applicants to be able to lift the weights specified. Entry requirements must be justifiable and not merely convenient.

3 Victimisation The third type of discrimination outlawed by the legislation is where someone is treated less favourably than other people by his employer because he has brought proceedings, given evidence or made allegations in good faith against his employer under the anti-discrimination legislation.

Segregation

The Race Relations Act also makes it illegal to segregate workers on racial grounds. Segregation by sex is not specifically prohibited.

Coverage of the anti-discrimination legislation

The Sex Discrimination and Race Relations Acts apply to all aspects of employment. In this chapter we examine in detail only their relevance to recruitment and selection decisions.

Recruitment

Employers must not unlawfully discriminate against potential employees in any of the following ways:

- in the general arrangements for filling a vacancy; for example, a supervisor should not tell a personnel officer to recruit 'a man to replace Charlie'.
- in deciding who to appoint to fill a vacancy; for example, by rejecting or omitting to consider applications from members of ethnic minorities.
- in offering different terms and conditions of employment depending on the sex or race of applicants; for example, by offering women lower rates of pay than men.

The most obvious effect of the Sex Discrimination Act in particular has been in the field of recruitment advertising. This is because of the requirement in the legislation that there should be nothing in the wording of advertisements to suggest that jobs are open to some groups and not to others.

Selection

The method of filling vacancies can be discriminatory. In the current recession, for example, there is evidence that organisations tend to use word-of-mouth as a recruitment method more frequently than previously. This is likely to perpetuate the status quo in that white males are likely to introduce other white males to fill vacant jobs. An investigation by the Commission for Racial Equality of a London firm of bakers and confectioners concluded that word-of-mouth recruitment was a form of indirect discrimination. Since many potential employees approach organisations by telephoning or calling in 'on spec', it is important that personnel department secretaries, receptionists and other employees in 'gatekeeping' roles understand their responsibilities in law.

Interviews are likely places for discriminatory behaviour. There may be a tendency for interviewers to attempt to replace a previous job incumbent with someone of similar outward characteristics. This may lead to a desire to eliminate interviewees who are outwardly dissimilar by 'proving' that they would be unable to cope with the demands of the job. Once, when I applied to a local authority for a lectureship in industrial relations which involved the running of courses for shop stewards, I was asked, 'As a woman, how would you deal with male shop stewards? After all they are rather peculiar animals!' Needless to say, male applicants were asked no similar question!

Indirect discrimination in recruitment

One of the most important cases so far has been *Price v. Civil Service Commission*. The case related to the age barrier of 28 for direct entry into the Executive Officer grade of the Civil Service. Belinda Price was 36. She claimed that her exclusion was indirect discrimination on the grounds of sex. Far fewer women than men could comply with this condition since, at this period of their lives, many women are out of the labour market, whilst raising children. It was accepted that it was desirable for the Civil Service to ensure that a proportion of external candidates entering the Executive Officer grade was drawn from the lower age groups to maintain a balanced career structure, but it was held that there were alternative, non-discriminatory ways of achieving this.

Genuine occupational qualifications (GOQ)

It is quite lawful to look for workers of a particular sex or racial group in order to fill well-defined jobs.

When being a man or a woman is a qualification for the job An example of a GOQ here would be lack of separate sleeping arrangements or toilet facilities, where the job requires employees to 'live in' and it would be unreasonable to ask the employer to provide alternative accommodation.

Self-check

List four further examples of jobs where sex is a GOQ.

ANSWER

- A female actor in a part written for a female character in a play.
- A female matron in an all-girls school.
- A male lavatory attendant in a men's toilet.
- A male chauffeur for a job in Saudi Arabia (where women are prohibited from driving by law).

Where race is a genuine occupational qualification for the job The principles here are the same as outlined above. An example would be a waiter in a Chinese restaurant.

It is up to management to justify the existence of a GOQ, if it is challenged by someone who feels unreasonably excluded from a job as a result.

Other groups protected from discriminatory recruitment decisions

Apart from the legislation prohibiting sex and race discrimination, there are only two other areas of statutory restriction on an employer's right to select employees.

Disabled workers Under the Disabled Persons (Employment) Act 1958 employers with more than twenty regular workers must ensure that they employ a quota of registered disabled workers (usually three per cent), unless an exempting permit has been issued to them. In addition, certain jobs, for example car park attendant, must not be filled by an able-bodied person unless no disabled person is available.

The Rehabilitation of Offenders Act 1974 Under this Act an individual is allowed to 'wipe out' some 'spent' offences after a specified period. Depending upon the sentence imposed, a conviction for an offence is said to be spent between six months and ten years after the offence was committed, provided that no further serious offence was committed during the rehabilitation period. Potential employees in this position need not normally disclose their spent conviction when applying for a job. However, this is not the case for doctors, dentists, opticians, vets, nurses, midwives, health or social workers, teachers, lawyers, legal clerks, accountants, policemen, probation officers or traffic wardens.

The contract of employment

Once the employer makes an offer of employment to an individual and this is accepted, a contract of employment comes into existence. This need not take the form of a written document, though it is customary for it to do so. The details of the contract are known as its terms and conditions. A contract of employment can be seen as an exchange of work for wages. For it to be a legal exchange, neither party should feel that they made the contract under duress and each should be free to enter into it. A contract of employment would lack legality, for example, if a boss threatened physically to harm a potential employee who refused an offer of employment. Also, if either side misrepresented themselves prior to the contract being agreed, the contract would be invalid. For example, if an applicant claimed to possess a qualification specified for entry to a job and subsequently this proved not to be so, the employer would be legally justified in dispensing with his services.

An employer must give each employee a written statement setting out the main particulars of the employment within thirteen weeks of the date of engagement.

Activity

Look at the written particulars of your own employment or, if you are not currently working, at someone else's. List ten items which appear in such a statement.

Your list should have included:

- Employer's name.
- Date employment began.
- Job title.
- Rate of pay (including overtime rates and annual increments).
- Hours of work.
- Holiday entitlement.
- Sick pay and procedures.
- Pension rights.
- Amounts of notice.
- Disciplinary and grievance procedures.

One thing you may have noticed was that several items were not specified in detail but reference was made to a place where the information could be found. Often this is a reference to a collective agreement. This is quite legal provided that the employee has a reasonable opportunity to read such a document.

This means that the employer need not notify employees individually of all changes in their terms and conditions of employment. However, management must inform workers that such changes will result, for example, from trade union negotiations and that they will be incorporated into subsequent written agreements with the trade unions. This is legitimate whether or not all workers belong to one of the trade unions which the organisation recognises for collective bargaining purposes.

The significance of the written statement

The written statement is not a contract of employment. As we said earlier, contracts of employment need not be in writing. However, if an employee does not receive written particulars of his employment within thirteen weeks of the date of engagement, or if he believes the document to be incorrect, he can take the matter to an industrial tribunal for an order that the employer should supply one. The written particulars are important to both parties, since either could experience a serious disadvantage in the courts, if a legal case arose out of the contract.

Not all workers must have written particulars by law. The major exclusions are:

- registered dock workers;
- husbands and wives of the employer;
- Crown and some National Health Service employees;
- employees who work wholly or mainly outside the UK;
- employees whose written particulars have already been embodied in a written contract; for example, as required in apprenticeship contracts.

Express and implied terms of a contract of employment

All contracts of employment contain 'express' conditions. These are those conditions which are expressed verbally or in writing. There are also 'implied' terms which are assumed to form part of every contract of employment under the common law. These are general obligations to be followed by employers and employees.

Employees' general obligations An employee's implied duties can be summarised as follows:

- to be ready and willing to work;
- to obey reasonable orders;
- to use reasonable care and skill;
- to conduct himself in the interest of the employer;
- to show good faith to his employer.

Employers' general obligations These include the duty:

- to pay agreed wages;
- not to make deductions from wages without employees' consent;
- to provide work (in some cases);
- to obey the law.

There is not space here to go into these obligations in detail. For further information see Chapter 4 of *Practical Business Law* by T.K. Price, Pan Breakthrough Books, 1982.

Review

What are the two main types of law which determine employees' rights at work?

ANSWER

- Statutory law.
- Case law.

As we saw earlier in the chapter, managers are mainly concerned with employees' statutory rights. These are sometimes called 'property' rights, since they are said to have established that workers have rights to occupy their job or property undisturbed and not to have it taken away without the operation of certain legal processes. In this sense it is argued that workers' rights, as regards the 'ownership' of their jobs, are analagous to the rights of individuals to other material possessions – houses, cars and other consumer goods, for example.

Another way of regarding legislation on the rights of the individual worker is to see it as a minimum 'floor' of rights. That is, many employers employ people on terms which are more favourable than those which the law requires them to provide. Often this occurs where collective bargaining has been highly developed for many years.

Summary – case study

To check your understanding of much of the subject matter of this chapter, I have written a case study, in which you are asked to examine the legal implications of a manager's actions in recruiting a new member of staff. Read it through and then answer the questions listed at the end.

Save Easy Building Society

John Baker is manager of the Middleford branch of the Save Easy Building Society. Middleford is a quiet but prosperous country market town with little manufacturing industry. The Save Easy Building Society is one of the country's largest building societies with offices in most major towns. Its smaller branches, of which the Middleford branch is typical, are staffed by a manager, usually male, and three or four part-time cashier/typists. The latter are usually married women, often with children, because the hours of work often suit their needs. One of John Baker's staff leaves and he needs to find a replacement. He places the following advertisement in the *Middleford Gazette*:

MUMS PLEASE NOTE!

THE SAVE EASY BUILDING SOCIETY
needs a
Part-time
Cashier/Typist

You will work mainly with the public, selling the Society's savings and mortgages services as well as answering telephone queries and general office duties. On-line computer terminals are used for cashiering and all necessary training is provided.

Would *you* like to be an important member of our team? Hours of work are 11.00 a.m. to 3.00 p.m. with additional hours as required (by mutual agreement). Saturday mornings are worked on a rota basis.

Please apply for an application form to: J. E. Baker, Branch Manager, Save Easy Building Society, 2 Golden Square, Middleford, MF1 1DT.

Six women telephone for application forms. From her voice, John deduces that one is black. He tells this applicant that the position has been filled. He feels justified in this action when he imagines the expressions on the faces of some of his clients if they were served by a black cashier. He would deny personal racial prejudice. When he was assistant manager of a branch in Pottington in the Midlands, he was happy to have black cashiers. But not here in Middleford! The clients would not be happy! Also, the job entails much telephone work and he found the applicant difficult to understand over the telephone.

Subsequently, four women complete application forms. One is fifty-five years old. He rejects her as too old for the job. With the advent of computer technology, she would not be able to cope. He notes that the other three applicants have school-age children and he calls them all for interview. From previous experience he has come to the conclusion that the most important characteristic of an effective member of staff is stability. People who leave disrupt efficiency. He is a man who likes a comfortable routine both in work and outside. He is a great believer in family life. It is most important that applicants have the support of their husbands and good childcare arrangements. Also, he likes to be sure that they are not going to have any more children. The prospect of having to recruit a temporary replacement to cover a period of maternity leave fills him with horror! It is therefore his normal practice, when he interviews applicants for jobs, to ask about these personal matters.

On this occasion one of the applicants objects to his questioning. She tells him that her private life is none of his business and promptly leaves the office. He reassures himself with the thought that she is some kind of cranky feminist.

The next interviewee has worked as a cashier in a large engineering company. This experience is probably relevant to the demands of work in the branch, he feels. However, further conversation reveals that she was a trade union representative in that company. Well, that rules her out – John Baker is decidedly opposed to having left-wing extremists working for him!

He offers the job to the third candidate, Mrs Susan Best, who starts work the following week. At the beginning of her second week John Baker gives the new employee a written statement of her main terms and conditions of employment. Since engaging Mrs Best, he has decided to change her hours of work a little so that she finishes work each day at 3.30 p.m. rather than 3.00 p.m. This change is incorporated into the statement and he tells her of his decision when he gives the document to her. She is most unhappy about the change, saying that this will make it impossible for her to meet her five-year-old son from school. He says that he is sorry but argues that the change is necessary in the interests of branch efficiency.

Work through this case study and comment on the correctness in law of John Baker's actions.

ANSWERS

1 The size of the Save Easy Building Society's Middleford branch office The Sex Discrimination Act applies only where there are more than six employees. However, though this office employs only four or five people, the building society is the employer in law and therefore the law applies to the situations described in this case. (No minimum size of firm is specified in the Race Relations Act 1976.)

2 The advertisement Under section 38 of the Sex Discrimination Act 1975, there should be nothing in the wording or presentation of advertisements for jobs to give the impression that only men or only women are required. Hence, John Baker's heading 'Mums please note', as well as being patronising in tone, is also illegal in that it implies that the vacancy is open only to female applicants.

3 The telephone enquiry The Race Relations Act 1976 specifies that individuals should not be treated less favourably than others on grounds of race. Only if John Baker could show that the exclusion of a black applicant was a genuine and necessary condition of employment, and not merely convenient, would his action be legal. His rationalisation about the feelings of his clientele *is* merely a convenience. His perception of the clarity of her intonation on the telephone *might* constitute reasonable grounds for rejection. However, the onus would be on him to prove *both* that clarity of expression was necessary, because of the amount and nature of the telephone work involved, *and* that the applicant did not measure up to the demands of the job in this respect.

4 Rejection of the fifty-five-year-old applicant This is legal. There is no age discrimination legislation in the UK. Interestingly, his action would have been illegal had his reason for rejection been proven in the United States.

5 Questioning about domestic circumstances According to the Sex Discrimination Act, John Baker should not treat applicants less favourably on grounds of sex or marriage than he treats or would treat other persons. If the female applicant in question had made a complaint to an industrial tribunal, John Baker would have been required to show that his questions indicated an intention to discriminate on grounds of parenthood rather than sex.

6 John Baker's concern about trade union activists His rejection of a candidate because of her past role as a trade union representative is quite legal. Applicants for jobs are not protected from discrimination on the grounds of trade union membership. Whilst his decision may be ethically suspect and unsound as a systematic selection decision, in law he is quite correct.

7 The change in Mrs Best's hours of work Under the Employment Protection (Consolidation) Act 1978, employers are required to give employees a written statement setting out the main terms and conditions of their employment. However, this statement is not the only facet of the contract of employment. The contract was made at the time that Mrs Best accepted the offer of a job as part-time cashier/typist. At that time the hours of work were as stipulated in the advertisement, i.e. 11.00 a.m. to 3.00 p.m. John Baker's decision to change them without her consent might be construed as constructive dismissal (see Chapter 15, p. 247). However, this is unlikely given the seemingly minor nature of the change.

In any case Mrs Best does not have one year's service (the current qualification period for unfair dismissal compensation – see p. 248). Therefore she cannot make a claim against him to an industrial tribunal. She could bring an action against him in the county court, but in view of her length of service any compensation would be likely to be minimal. The court would be unlikely to order her reinstatement. If other similar work was difficult to find, she would probably choose to stay, and after arguing, put up with the change. However, such an unhelpful or even dishonest way of managing staff is unlikely to lead to harmonious working relationships and an efficient office.

6 | Involving the individual in the job

In the previous chapters we examined the process by which individuals are brought into the organisation. At this time attempts are made to select employees with the potential to perform jobs effectively. Whether or not employees live up to the expectations of those who selected them depends on management's success in motivating them to work effectively. In other words:

capability × motivation = *performance.*

Though this equation is oversimplified, it stresses the centrality of motivation to the employment relationship. Personnel specialists are charged with responsibility to find this 'philosopher's stone' or means of resolving management's problems, so far as employees are concerned. The next few chapters look at techniques aimed at increasing the effectiveness of workers. In this chapter we are concerned with the general nature of motivation to work and its relationship to techniques concerned with the management of people.

Motivation

Probably no subject has taxed the energy of management pundits more than motivation to work. Many famous theories now exist for the guidance of managers. Unfortunately they are often contradictory.

Activity

Here is a list of factors which may affect your feelings about your job. Rank them in order of importance to you personally. Put 1 against the factor that is most important to you, 2 against the next and so on.

1 Security of employment
2 Promotion prospects
3 Salary or wage
4 Personal relationships at work
5 Life outside work
6 Physical working conditions
7 Interesting work
8 Challenging work
9 Opportunities to be creative at work
10 Status
11 Fringe benefits or 'perks'
12 Recognition of a job well done

Of course there is no right or wrong answer to this activity. Your answer will depend on such things as:

- the job that you do;
- your age;
- your experience of life and work;
- your hopes for the future.

A further complication is that your feelings about work may change from time to time. For example, whilst you are doing your job you may be concerned that it is challenging and interesting and gives you opportunities to be creative. When the union which represents you is negotiating the next pay increase, you may be more concerned about the money you are paid.

Ask friends or colleagues to do the above exercise. The variety of their answers and the discussions which you have with them afterwards should further convince you of the complexity of this area.

Do employees work for love or money?

The research evidence is contradictory. Some research subjects stress the importance of pay. By contrast the majority of workers seem convinced that they would continue to work if they inherited a fortune or won the football pools. There is anecdotal evidence to support this from workers who have found themselves lucky enough to be able to make this choice. Clearly for them money is not the only source of motivation!

Before looking at the social scientists' explanations for this seemingly contradictory evidence, we should pause and think about the effect on the behaviour of managers. Many have their 'pet' theories about ways of encouraging employees to work harder. This affects the personnel management techniques chosen to this end.

Self-check

Suppose you believe that workers are most likely to perform effectively if their work is interesting. What techniques are you likely to use in the hope of increasing productivity?

The answer is techniques which involve redesigning jobs to make them intrinsically more interesting.

By contrast, if you believe that an attractive working environment is vital to workers' motivation, you may spend much time selecting attractive potted plants and designing colour schemes!

Most managements have traditionally operated on a 'carrot and stick' theory of motivation, believing that provision of appropriate incentives, particularly money, encourages workers to expend the maximum effort. This is the theory behind many payment systems (see Chapter 12). Support for this thesis can be derived from the nature of our consumer society. Not surprisingly workers have materialistic values; those who perform dull jobs may have little else than money by which to be motivated!

Maslow's hierarchy of needs

This is the most famous classification of human needs based on the assumption that people have wants directed to specific goals. Maslow postulated five main categories of need arranged in a *hierarchy* _ i.e. once a lower order need is satisfied, the individual becomes motivated by needs which exist at the next highest level of the hierarchy.

In figure 15 we see that Maslow assumed that, if people have enough to eat and drink, their attention turns to the need for security – the tramp's dream for a roof over his head or the

Figure 15. Maslow's hierarchy of needs

worker's concern to avoid redundancy. Once this is satisfied, attention turns to relationships with other people – the need to feel wanted and loved. At this stage workers are concerned with their membership of a work group and of an organisation. The higher-order needs for self-esteem or status and recognition in the eyes of the world, and finally for self-actualisation or the achievement of full potential, become motivators only when the lower order needs have been satisfied.

Self-check

Do employees cease to be concerned about money once their basic needs have been met?

You probably answered 'no', since we can all think of people who earn a great deal of money but whose negotiating behaviour demonstrates that they are far from satisfied. As indicated earlier, the reason for this seems to lie in the nature of our consumer society. A complication of Maslow's theory seems to be that money is a means of satisfying needs at most levels of the hierarchy.

Self-check

Can you think of another problem in applying Maslow's hierarchy?

Earlier we discussed the fact that employees seem to be motivated by different aspects of jobs in different situations. Thus, on the same day, they may demand more money in a negotiating meeting and more satisfying work on the job. It seems that two or more levels of the hierarchy may operate at the same time.

Despite these criticisms, Maslow's hierarchy has value for managers and personnel specialists, suggesting that:

- the nature of the motivation to work is complex;
- there is no single overriding source of motiviation;
- managers or personnel specialists cannot afford to 'rest on their laurels', having given workers a generous pay increase for example. Demands at a higher level in the hierarchy should be anticipated.

Herzberg's 'two factor' theory of motivation

In the view of this American organisational psychologist, the wants of employees can be divided into *satisfiers* or motivators and *dissatisfiers* or 'hygiene' factors. The first group are said to be effective motivators because they are a source of personal growth. They include:

- achievement;
- recognition;
- advancement;
- responsibility; and
- the work itself.

By contrast, as indicated by the terminology, the presence of 'hygiene' factors prevents dissatisfaction and poor performance. In other words, such aspects of job context must be present if the employee is to feel fairly treated. Hygiene factors include:

- wages or salaries;
- supervision;
- working conditions; and
- company policy and administration.

These factors do not act as motivators, but if they are not present or are felt by employees to be inadequate, they will act as a source of dissatisfaction.

> *Self-check*
>
> According to Herzberg, is money a source of motivation to work?

No. This is one of the 'hygiene' factors. Employees must feel the level of their remuneration is fair for the job they are asked to do if this is not to be a source of dissatisfaction. However, even if employees are paid much more than the market rate, this will not be a source of motivation.

Like Maslow's hierarchy of needs, this theory has been accused of being overgeneralised and too simplified. Nevertheless it provides food for thought in its message that, no matter how satisfactory the context of the job, if the work itself is dull and meaningless, the employee will be apathetic.

Orientations to work

Psychologists focus on the needs and wants of the individual employee at work. Sociologists, by contrast, analyse the degree to which wider social forces impinge on the work behaviour of employees. To understand workers' attitudes and values, we need to know what workers expect from and value in their work. The term 'orientation to work' is used to categorise employees' preferences about various features and rewards of work. In a famous study, John Goldthorpe* identified the prevalence of an 'instrumental' orientation to work among highly paid manual workers. These people tended to see work as a means to an end, a way of earning a living to support an affluent lifestyle outside work. For them work was not a central life interest.

> *Self-check*
>
> Goldthorpe's evidence suggests that the employees concerned were prepared to put up with dull, repetitive jobs, for example on car assembly lines, as long as the financial rewards were satisfactory. Does this contradict the findings of the organisational psychologists?

*J. H. Goldthorpe *et al.*, *The Affluent Worker: Industrial Attitudes and Behaviour*, Cambridge University Press, 1968.

The answer is that, of course, the organisational psychologists would refuse to accept that money can be a major motivator for highly paid workers. However, they would be prepared to see it as a symbol of success and affluence in life generally and of recognition at work. Thus money may satisfy several intangible needs.

A further argument for Goldthorpe's findings lies in the nature of the employment relationship. This is predominantly an exchange of wages for effort. Thus it is hardly surprising if employees see work largely in calculative terms. Goldthorpe's affluent workers and many others like them receive little from their work other than financial rewards. An absence of positive or moral commitment is not remarkable.

Nevertheless sociologists have identified other orientations to work. For example some employees have a bureaucratic attachment to the organisations in which they work. These are mainly white-collar workers who have some expectation of upward movement through the organisation structure. For them career development is very important and work is a central life interest. Involvement in work is moral rather than simply calculative. Some employees are 'cosmopolitans' in that they see themselves not as employees of a particular organisation but as members of a professional or occupational group. That is, the major group with which they identify is outside the firm rather than inside it. For them too work is a central life interest but their orientation is to opportunities in the labour market generally rather than within the organisation in which they happen to be currently employed.

Review

Identify three lessons for managers and personnel specialists in the work of social scientists in the area of motivation and orientations to work.

ANSWERS

- The relationship between individuals and their work is complex. Managers and personnel specialists should not assume that any change of employment policy or practice will provoke the same response from all employees.

- Employees' attitudes and priorities may change over time and in different circumstances. A key skill which you will need as a manager or personnel specialist is to put yourself in other people's shoes and see work through their eyes.
- Know yourself! Be aware of your own assumptions and 'pet' theories which influence your dealings with other people at work.

Designing jobs to encourage efficiency and commitment

Self-check

Suppose you need to decide on the content of a shop assistant's job in terms of its duties and responsibilities. List two objectives which you would have in making these decisions.

ANSWER

- The requirements of the business for productivity and quality of service.
- The needs of the job holder for satisfying work.

Management has tended to give much greater priority to the first objective than to the second. The resultant lack of involvement of employees in decisions relating to them and their consequent lack of motivation has prompted a debate about the quality of working life. (Part of this debate is about the need for greater employee participation in managerial decision-making, see Chapter 14.)

Self-check

List three effects of highly specialised and routine jobs on employees.

- They do not satisfy needs for personal fulfilment and growth.
- Research undertaken in the USA indicates that those who perform machine-paced specialised assembly jobs suffer from particularly high levels of psychological strain and somatic

complaints. Stress is not restricted to those who occupy managerial roles.

- They do not use employees' full abilities; they are frustrating and may encourage participation in unproductive acts ranging from shoddy work to literally throwing a spanner in the works; they can result in absenteeism, wildcat strikes and refusal to cooperate with management.

In times of full employment, the dislike of these jobs by many members of the labour force meant that employers had recruitment difficulties. In Sweden this led to the famous experiment in work restructuring at Volvo Cars. Management also has had difficulties in getting employees to accept technological change because of fears that it threatens the narrow range of skills on which they depend for a living.

Efforts to create a more positive commitment by employees have affected only a small proportion of the labour force. This shows how deep-rooted are employers' assumptions about the link between specialised, narrow tasks and high producitvity. Our analysis of the effect of such jobs on employees should at least emphasise the value of experiments in the area of job redesign.

What are the options in redesigning jobs?

Activity

You are a personnel specialist in a large supermarket chain. Many problems which can be categorised as poor motivation to work have been experienced with checkout operators. List three options for redesigning this job.

- You could include one or more other tasks at the same level of difficulty within the operator's job. For example, if another assistant packs customers' shopping while the checkout operator enters prices into the till, you could give one person responsibility for both tasks. This addition of related tasks is known as 'job enlargement'.
- Another option is 'job rotation', whereby all assistants are moved between various routine tasks in the store such as shelf

filling, checkout operating and, where relevant, serving customers on specialist counters.

- The third option needs more radical redesign of the job to add elements involving more responsibility in decision-making. This probably would involve adding elements of the job of first-line supervisors for signing cheques, exchanging faulty goods and dealing with customer complaints. It also might involve the work group becoming more overtime. The term used to describe this is 'job enrichment'.

Elements of the first two options would be found in many supermarkets since they are much more congruent with the philosophy of 'don't do as you think, do as you're told'. They have been criticised as merely 'adding one Mickey Mouse job to another'. There is evidence that where workers favour enlargement or rotation, fatigue and boredom have been reduced. However, there is little evidence of productivity improvements and once the new tasks become familiar the motivational effect often wears off. Sometimes employees have expressed dislike of job rotation because it breaks up established work groups and thus reduces opportunities for the development of social relationships at work.

Job enrichment By contrast, job enrichment is said to create opportunities for increased performance and satisfaction. Job enrichment generally has three elements:

- Reduced repetitiveness of work.
- Incorporation of some of the activitvies of related jobs into the enriched jobs. In the case of manual jobs this often involves responsibility for reordering of stock, inspection of maintenance.
- Delegation of decision-making to employees. Again in the case of manual workers this may involve responsibility for scheduleing and planning their own work.

  Trade unions argue that increases in responsibility must be compensated by financial rewards. Workers do not live by job satisfaction alone!

Self-check

List two other problems which job enrichment may present for management.

ANSWER

- Initial investment costs may be substantial. This applied, for example, to the new manufacturing techniques introduced by Volvo Cars in Sweden.
- The evidence suggests that there may be an initial drop in productivity as people adjust to new jobs.

Other costs may be incurred too; for example, workers are likely to need training for more complex restructured jobs.

Benefits have been claimed in organisations where work restructuring has taken place. Reduced labour turnover and absenteeism, improvements in both quality and quantity of work and more intangible improvements in employee relations and job satisfaction have been reported elsewhere. Certainly, the long-term gains from job enrichment are difficult to measure, being related to overall organisational performance.

Direct participation as a means of encouraging employee commitment

Job enrichment gives opportunities for employees to contribute to decisions about work they perform. It is a form of direct employee participation in organisation decision-making (see Chapter 14 pp. 236–7).

Self-check

Imagine you are an employee of Byteman Computer Services. The company has 1,000 employees in four locations in the UK. Employees are unionised. There is bargaining at company level between management and trade unions. A joint consultative committee draws employee representatives from all four sites. There are no other mechanisms for employee participation in managerial decision-making. Do

> you think these systems would increase your commitment
> to and involvement in the company and your own job?

Such systems of indirect participation, if seen as fair and effective
by employees, might increase your general satisfaction with your
terms and conditions of employment. Likewise, if through your
representatives on the joint consultative committee you receive
information on company plans and the current situation, you
might feel more positive towards your employment by Byteman.
However, research shows that such efforts to introduce participation at the highest levels alone run the risk that only at election
times do employees feel involved in organisational affairs.

This is the argument for direct participation. Such experiments
have been small-scale in the UK. Long-established methods of
collective bargaining and consultation have been more prevalent. Experience suggests that the recognised framework of
employee participation in managerial decision-making –
the union-management relationship – must not be neglected
and newer methods of participation should not seek to replace
traditional unionised representation.

Methods of direct participation
These include:

- autonomous work groups;
- quality circles;
- suggestion schemes.

> ### Review
>
> What method of direct participation already discussed in
> this chapter is omitted from the above list?

ANSWER

Job enrichment and other methods of work restructuring.

Autonomous work groups These are an extension of job enrichment in which members of a work group are given limited responsibility for immediate production planning and for task allocation arrangements. Most of the experiments in this form of

employee participation have occurred in Scandinavia. At Volvo, the car assembly line was scrapped to provide a more favourable environment for group working. However, whilst increases in organisational efficiency have been noted in these experiments, the degree to which management has relinquished control of production is limited. That is, though workers have taken over some of the functions of first-line supervisors, managers above this level have renounced little of their decision-making powers.

Review

What was the major reason for introducing group working and job enrichment in Scandinavian organisations such as Volvo?

You should have remembered that, in our discussion of job enrichment, we said management was concerned with the unattractiveness of repetitive specialised jobs. When there was little unemployment, recruitment difficulties and higher labour turnover resulted. The experiments in group working and job enrichment were an attempt to solve these problems.

Quality circles These have been imported into the UK as part of the attempt to make our industry more competitive by learning from the Japanese. Supervisors and work groups are provided with training in quality control and other problem-solving techniques. They are encouraged then to attempt to identify and solve work-related problems using specialist advice where necessary.

Self-check

Dynamic Machines is a large UK manufacturer of aeroengines. Having secured the agreement of the general manager to the launch of a trial quality circle, the quality manager has designed a training programme for those involved, with the help of the training department. Now he is ready to choose a department in which to locate the circle. List three criteria which he should use in making the choice.

ANSWER

- Management, supervisors and employees in the department must be enthusiastic to participate in the trial.
- Industrial relations in the department must be good and trade union representatives should be willing to participate in the circle.
- Departmental management must be known to be willing and able to listen carefully and responsively to employee proposals.

> *Self-check*
>
> Do you think a method of participation adopted from another culture – in this case Japan – is likely to be successful in this country?

In Chapter 1 we emphasised that no universal principles govern the practice of personnel management. Management and personnel specialists should take care in shaping policies and practices suitable to their own organisation and culture. It may be, though, that we can identify some key similarities between Japan and the UK which account for the success of quality circles in some British companies. These are:

- rising aspirations and increased education of workers;
- the need to reduce the specialised and routine nature of many production and clerical jobs;
- the need to increase the commitment of many employees both to the organisation and to the jobs they perform within it.

Nevertheless many differences exist between the employment relationship in Japan and in the UK which should prompt managers and personnel specialists to pause for thought before launching quality circles or any other aspect of Japanese personnel management.

Suggestion schemes Our last example of schemes of direct employee participation has been established far longer than work restructuring, autonomous work groups or quality circles. However, only rarely have suggestion schemes been effective in involving employees in organisational decision-making. This is because traditionally employees have not been involved in either the design or operation of these schemes and feel that the decision-making process about the acceptance or rejection of their suggestions is remote from them. Frequently such decisions are made by a committee of managers with no obligation to tell the initiators of suggestions the reason for their decision. The committee may take time in communicating the results of its deliberations. Further, managers and supervisors often feel that suggestions made by those for whom they are responsible are implicitly critical of their performance. Conflict can also arise over the size of the monetary or other reward for the submission of a successful suggestion.

Self-check

Taking into account the problems encountered in the running of suggestion schemes, list four criteria for the establishment of a successful scheme.

ANSWER

- Commitment of all levels of management.
- Involvement and support of recognised trade unions.
- Involvement of employees during the evaluation of their suggestions.
- Active support of departmental management, supervisory and specialist support staff in the operation of the scheme. It should be clear that the emergence of suggestions is not a criticism of their competence.

You may also have noted that it is useful to have an administrator for the scheme – probably a personnel specialist, who services the committee, monitors the scheme, organises training and generally performs a coordinating role.

Review

Which of the following statements are true and which are false?

1 'Money is the only effective motivator of employees.'
  True or false?
2 'Managers and supervisors should not assume that any
  change of employment policy or practice will provoke
  the same response from all employees.' *True or false?*
3 'Job rotation, job enlargement and job enrichment are
  all methods of work restructuring.' *True or false?*
4 'Quality circles are a long-established method of direct
  employee participation, which originated in the UK.'
  True or false?
5 'There are many effective suggestion schemes in UK
  companies.' *True or false?*

ANSWERS

1 False.
2 True.
3 True.
4 False.
5 False.

7 | Appraising performance

'Getting the best out of people' is a crude expression of management's key target so far as employees are concerned. In the last chapter we examined the general issue of employee motivation. Performance appraisal, the subject of this chapter, rests on the assumption that if employees' performance is scrutinised and feedback is given, the motivation to work more effectively should increase. Problems of employee motivation where this is not done or done badly can be expressed as 'the good people don't know what they should be doing or how well they are doing' and 'nobody finds out the bad people'.

In this chapter we look at ways of righting such situations using performance appraisal.

What is performance appraisal?

The dictionary definition of the verb *to appraise* is 'to fix a price for' or 'to value an object or thing'. When we use the term 'performance appraisal' we imply that we are concerned with the process of valuing the employee's worth to the organisation, with a view to increasing it.

Purpose of performance appraisal

Self-check

List three of management's objectives in appraising employees' performance.

ANSWER

- To help improve current performance.
- To assess training and development needs.
- To assess future potential for promotion.

You may have also listed:

- To give employees feedback on their performance.
- To counsel employees on career opportunities.
- To rate the employees' performance for salary review purposes.

This latter is controversial. I recommend that 'reward reviews' are separated from appraisal. The association with monetary reward tends to cause over-concentration on this area at the expense of the mutual attempt by manager and employee to identify training needs, improve current performance and possible future potential.

Who is appraised?

Managerial, professional and technical staff trainees are more likely to be appraised than holders of routine clerical and manual jobs. One reason for this is the association between appraisal and training and career development.

Designing an appraisal system

Self-check

You are managing director of XYZ Systems Ltd. Your main competitor ABC Systems Ltd employs roughly the same number and skills-mix of employees as you. You wish to begin to use a performance appraisal system. ABC has such a system. Should you attempt to cajole your counterpart in ABC to let you have this system?

Aside from the unreality of this in that your main rival is unlikely to let you have anything which might make you more competitive, the answer is probably 'no'. It is generally unwise to attempt to transfer systems concerned with the management of people from one organisation to another, however tempting this may appear. Appraisal systems like other aspects of personnel management must suit the company culture. Even though ABC is your main competitor it may differ in tradition, methods of dealing with employees, structure and organisation of work and so on.

If you believe that an appraisal system can contribute to the efficient running of XYZ you would be better advised to 'grow your own'. To do this it is useful to use the experience of others. A summary of trends in performance appraisal shows:

- increasing criticism of appraisal systems which attempt to measure personality characteristics such as intelligence, loyalty, commitment or drive;
- increased emphasis on more objective, job-related criteria and objectives – a 'results-oriented approach';
- more involvement of employees in their own appraisal;
- more concentration on improving performance in the current job rather than assessing future potential.

We shall examine each of these in turn.

Personality-based appraisal systems

> *Self-check*
>
> Can managers make judgements about their subordinates on such dimensions as intelligence, initiative or loyalty?

The answer must be 'With difficulty!' To illustrate this point let us use the example of a manager who is asked to rate the intelligence of his subordinates:

- Firstly, he must understand what intelligence is.
- Secondly, he must be competent to judge the degree to which it exists in other people.
- Thirdly, can he assume that all his subordinates exhibit all their intelligence in their jobs? For example, if you give an intelligent adult a task to do which would only test the intelligence of a ten-year-old, is it fair to judge his intelligence by his job performance?
- Fourthly, he must assess all his subordinates in the same way against his definition of intelligence.
- Fifthly, if he is required to give feedback to his employee on the results of the appraisal, and increasingly this is the case, he

may find it difficult to justify an assessment based on personality trait rating.

In addition, studies have shown that, whatever the chosen personality characteristic appraisal was likely to reveal, women and members of other minority groups emerge as having less of it than their white male counterparts. The existence of anti-discrimination legislation thus makes it unwise to use appraisal systems which have the effect of treating employees of one sex or race less favourably than other people in decisions which relate to promotion (see Chapter 11, pp. 175–6). In appraisal as in selection, the roots of prejudice tend to be very close to the surface.

Results-oriented appraisal systems or performance reviews

It follows that fair judgements of performance must be:

- capable of more objective judgement by appraisers;
- genuinely related to job performance.

This justifies an emphasis on job-related performance criteria. Our next step is to find the most appropriate measures of job performance.

Activity

Discuss the content of his job with someone who is a manager, supervisor, professional or technical employee. Seek a full impression of what is done. Then try together to think of three ways of establishing criteria of effective performance for purposes of appraisal. You should not try to think what those criteria might be but rather what sort of information you would need and how you could collect it.

Three general methods of deriving such performance measures are:

- analysis of work content – documents, files, etc.;
- questionnaire about job performance;
- analysis of key problems experienced by job holders.

Analysis of work content If you were designing a performance review system for personnel specialists you could look at documents produced by them – interview reports, training programmes, records of negotiations with trade unions and so on.

It would be necessary to establish the key skills in drawing up such documents. For the job of a personnel specialist this might include:

- clarity of expression;
- conciseness;
- methodical storage of information;
- logical structure of reports.

However, by no means all the work of such specialists consists of written records. A great deal of time is spent talking to other people in interviews and meetings, formal or informal. Therefore the content of such exchanges can also be analysed for key skills.

Questionnaires about job performance Personnel specialists and their managers can be asked to complete questionnaires to describe the most and least effective performer in this job. Detailed statistical analysis of a number of such questionnaires should give a profile of an effective specialist, against which individuals' actual job performance can be measured.

Analysis of key problems of job holders Specialists or their managers can be asked to describe the most difficult problem they have experienced recently at work. This is often called the critical incident method. After a large number of such incidents have been collected they are analysed for trends, commonality and so on. These too can then be used to identify key skills.

Rating performance using job-related measures

Key criteria of performance thus established become yardsticks against which managers are asked to rate subordinates. Often rating scales are used for this purpose.

Self-check

Imagine you are a manager in a company which has used a combination of the three methods discussed above to establish criteria of effective performance. You are asked to use this rating scale to assess your subordinates against the criteria:

1 Excellent.
2 Very good.
3 Adequate.
4 Below the required standard.

This scale has only one category for ineffective performance. Why do you think this is?

Managers are usually required to communicate their evaluation of performance to subordinates. Imagine your disillusionment if you were labelled as 'inadequate' or 'below standard' in this way. Possibly you would live up to your reputation! Better to place only the most unsatisfactory employees in this category. Management is more likely to encourage employees to improve by jointly agreeing how they can be helped to improve, for example by further training and development.

Another problem of rating scales is that managers' definitions of 'excellent', 'very good' and so on may differ. Only trained appraisers using common yardsticks should use them.

Job-related objectives

Many experienced practitioners argue that performance reviews are more effective motivators if they involve the setting of specific job-related objectives. Six or so key performance measures can be selected at the appraisal interview as relevant target areas for the employee for the next year. These can then be turned into specific objectives.

For example, a key performance measure for a training specialist might be: 'the design and implementation of management development programmes'. An objective for a particular trainer might be 'to investigate the detailed training needs of line managers in accountancy and finance, to design a short course (not more than five days' duration) and to run three such courses each for twelve line managers within the next six months'.

> ## Self-check
>
> List three advantages of this objective setting procedure for use in performance reviews.

ANSWERS

● It should be relevant to the personal needs of the employee. Therefore his commitment should be greater.

● It should be relevant to the requirements of the job and of the organisation.

● It encourages both appraiser and appraised to look carefully at what has actually been achieved in the immediate past as well as what realistically may be expected over the year ahead.

Employee involvement in appraisal

Appraisal systems are now more 'open' than they used to be. That is, there is a greater likelihood that employees will be shown either all or a part of their appraisal reports. This should increase employees' motivation to improve their job performance.

Many managers find 'open' appraisal threatening. This is because there is pressure on the appraiser to make the appraisal as complete and constructive as possible. Bland phrases and generalisations are likely to be challenged by employees together with the more obvious inaccuracies which indicate the manager's ignorance of the real nature of the employee's job.

The trend towards more openness has been accompanied by greater emphasis on results-oriented approaches. It is easier to justify assessment of performance based on the key results areas of the job rather than on more nebulous, and less obviously relevant, personality traits.

Current performance v. future potential

Many managers do not see assessment of potential as a prime

purpose of appraisal. In the present recession many companies have reduced the size of their labour force.

|| *Self-check*

|| What are the implications of such a reduction for the career
|| development of existing employees?

There will be fewer opportunities for upward movement.

Many companies now encourage people to make sideways moves to increase their experience, knowledge and skills before or instead of upward progression. As a result, performance appraisal is concerned more with current performance than with future potential.

Potential reviews

Separate systematic reviews of potential are useful for those for whom career or management development is contemplated. Many managers find the assessment of potential difficult since their experience of the individual is limited to observations of performance in their current job. For this reason a 'grandfather' figure – a more senior manager – is often used to avoid some of the prejudices of the immediate manager. Another way of assessing potential is to use an assessment centre (see Chapter 9, pp. 149–51).

Who will appraise?

So far in this chapter we have implied that appraisal is commonly undertaken by the immediate supervisor. This is most often the case. Sometimes, as mentioned in the previous section, a more senior manager is used in an overseeing role. More open appraisal implies a shift in the control of appraisal from the appraiser to the appraisee. Some companies use self-appraisal schemes where the employee takes the lead. This may be useful where employees' work is frequently unsupervised and elements of it are not easily assessable; for example, professional employees. In similar circumstances, peer group appraisal can be used, where each employee nominates one or two colleagues whom he trusts to evaluate his performance. However, in most organisations managers prefer to retain control of appraisal.

Other problems of appraisal

A now classic research study* revealed that:

- managers are often reluctant to appraise subordinates;
- where they do, their written comments are often glib, generalised and evasive.

Three reasons can be suggested for this:

- managers often find appraisal schemes cumbersome and suspect that little action will be taken on the results;
- often managers lack training in appraisal;
- in life we are often reluctant to tell others how we feel about them. Why should we behave any differently at work?

Such research findings have led some people to see performance appraisal as a 'ritual of employment' without real benefit to either management or employees.

> *Activity*
>
> Talk to someone who has participated in appraisal in the last year either as appraiser or appraisee. (Or if yourself have had such an experience, use this.) Discuss the advantages and disadvantages of appraisal. Then list three points in favour and three points against.

There are no right or wrong answers. Much depends on the nature of the organisation, the appraisal system and the skills of those involved. My list is meant to trigger further thought.

Advantages

- In an appraisal interview boss and subordinate have a formal opportunity for a candid exchange of views, provided that the

*Kay Rowe, 'An appraisal of appraisals, *Journal of Management Studies*, volume 1, no.1, March 1964.

relationship between them and the nature of the appraisal scheme encourage this.

- Good performance appraisal systems encourage line managers to think systematically about career and management development for their subordinates.
- Performance appraisal can provide very useful data for the analysis of training needs and the design of training programmes.

Disadvantages

- The relationship between boss and subordinate is frequently fragile. It can be harmed by the necessity for the manager to formulate in words, written or spoken, what he really feels about his subordinate. In the words of one appraisee after an appraisal interview, 'I went in bruised and came out bleeding.'
- Even after training, some managers have difficulty with appraisal interviews.
- Many appraisal systems involve too much paperwork. This hinders rather than helps.

Conditions necessary for successful appraisal schemes

Despite all the criticism, the evidence is that the popularity of appraisal has not declined. Over 70 per cent of organisations have appraisal systems and most of those which do not are small companies, where the process probably occurs informally.

So are there any general lessons to be learnt before introducing an appraisal system? Careful analysis of the organisation's particular circumstances is vital before embarking on this difficult path. Here are ten suggestions:

- Get top management support.
- Plan and prepare carefully.
- Beware glossy consultancy packages or some other company's scheme.
- Give oral introductory presentations to managers, trade union representatives and employees.
- Prepare explanatory pamphlets for all those involved.
- Train appraisers.

- Make sure that the scheme is effectively implemented.
- Ensure that promises made in appraisal interviews, for example for further training, are carried out.
- Avoid close linkage with pay.
- Closely monitor the operation of the scheme.

Lastly, keep it simple! If a vast bureaucracy can be avoided, avoid it. Some companies have found that the key to successful appraisal lies in the appraisal interview. In a review of performance using key results areas only, a written record of those and of the associated objectives for the year ahead, together with any training needs, are vital.

Review – a cautionary tale

George has been test department manager in an engineering company for the last ten years. He sees the personnel department as a source of incessant gimickry, particularly on performance appraisal. Systems come and systems go and all complicate his relationship with his subordinates. He fails to complete his appraisal forms when he can get away with it. At present the personnel manager has the ear of the production director and George has been given an edict to undertake appraisal for all trainees, technicians, engineers and supervisors. The current appraisal system contains the following elements:

- agreement of key objectives for the year ahead between appraiser and appraisee;
- personality trait assessment of such characteristics as decision-making ability, leadership ability, alertness and mental capability, commitment, loyalty;
- assessment of potential on a rating scale – promotable in the near future / possibly promotable / not promotable;
- training and development needs.

George obediently completes the forms and sends them back to the personnel department thinking it a useless exercise but at least that will be that for another year. Then to his annoyance a young graduate personnel officer, whom George considers still 'wet behind the ears', telephones to inform George that the exercise is incomplete. The system now requires interviews to be conducted to communicate the results of appraisal to employees. George agrees to do this, suspecting that it is futile to argue. He is not happy with some of his assessments of personality in particular and has rated 50 per cent of those appraised as not promotable. This won't go down too well he knows but the firm has been reducing its labour force and promotion does consist of waiting for dead men's shoes. Presumably the personnel department, with its fancy knowledge of human behaviour, knows what it's doing!

He calls in each of his subordinates, reads the form to them and, not very enthusiastically, waits for a response.

Questions

1 List three failings by the personnel department in this case.
2 How effective do you think George's appraisal interviews would be?

ANSWERS

1   i Failure to brief George adequately on the purpose of appraisal schemes, and in the past, presumably to monitor the operation of appraisal systems.

  ii Failure to train George in appraisal, including interviewing techniques.

 iii Failure to ask George how he had managed to complete the 'key objectives' section of the form prior to the interview!

   You could also have queried the wisdom of requiring George to undertake personality trait rating and to communicate his assessment of potential to employees.

2 Remember the quotation at the beginning of this chapter: 'the good people don't know what they should be doing or how, well they are doing' and 'nobody finds out the bad people'. In addition, the communication of their perceived lack of potential to many employees increased dissatisfaction and had an adverse effect on production. A cautionary tale indeed!

8 | Training for current jobs

What is training?

From childhood we learn to cope with living. Is this training, or is it education? These terms are often used as if they were synonymous. They are not, and an understanding of the differences between them is important to an understanding of the training process in business organisations. Both are processes which help people to learn but they differ in orientation and objectives. It is probably simplest to define training as oriented towards the needs of the organisation whilst education is oriented to the needs of the individual. These differences can be summarised as shown in figure 16.

You will see from figure 16 that, whilst there are many contrasts between them, the line between training and education is sometimes very blurred. This is easy to see if we examine the content of qualification courses designed to develop managers. Some aspects of such programmes can be described as training since they enable intending or practising managers to develop specific skills, such as interviewing or computer programming, of direct relevance to current or future jobs; other aspects are more broadly educational such as the analysis of the perspectives of the parties in industrial relations or of the social context of work organisations. Such courses should contain elements of both education and training if employees are to be fully competent to contribute to the achievement of corporate objectives.

Objectives of training

Self-check

List two objectives of the training process in a work organisation.

Characteristics of the learning process	Education	Training
Objectives	More abstract objectives geared to the needs of the individual and to society generally	Specific behaviourial objectives to make workers more effective in their jobs
Timescale	Generally a long-term process	Can be very short-term especially when concerned with the acquisition of specific skills
Content	Widely drawn content	Often fairly narrow content specific to the employee's work situation

Figure 16. Differences between education and training

- To assist workers to perform at the optimum level in current jobs.
- To develop employees for future jobs.

Training policy

To supply the organisation with effective manpower, the training function must be acquainted with or involved in the corporate planning process. Training policies must be related to and supportive of corporate policies.

Fred's Food Processing Company, a manufacturer of frozen foods, plans to acquire a chain of frozen food shops over the next two years. The company's training function needs to be involved in the implementation of this decision, so that, when the retail business is acquired, there is a trained labour force to run it. Fred intends to recruit an entirely new workforce for the retail operation. Here is Fred's training policy.

Fred's Food Processing Company

Statement of training policy

The aim of this policy is to ensure that all employees are assisted to develop themselves in order that they may make the best possible contribution to the achievement of company objectives.

In the training area it is our policy to :

1 Draw up a training plan with reference to company objectives.
2 Involve managers in the identification of training objectives for their units.
3 Base training on a thorough analysis of needs.
4 Provide employees with potential with opportunities for further training and development.
5 Have a specialist training department charged with responsibility for the development and implementation of training plans.
6 Provide induction training for all employees.
7 Provide day release for first qualification training for all staff between the ages of 16 and 25.
8 Provide training courses and other training facilities to satisfy needs identified by managers or specialist training staff.
9 All training will be funded from the training budget and must be authorised by the head of the training department.

Self-check

What element in this policy statement is inconsistent with Fred's plans to move into retailing?

Item **4** does not fit with Fred's intention to recruit workers for the shops from the open market. Actions in breach of declared policy are likely to be very damaging to employee morale. Fred should advertise new posts within the manufacturing company before attempting to recruit new employees, unless he wishes to change this aspect of company policy.

A systematic approach to training

Training can contribute to the effective use of the organisation's resources, but only if approached systematically.

Activity

You are the owner of a shop. You recruit a school leaver as a trainee shop assistant. What questions would you need to ask yourself before starting to train the young person?

ANSWER

- What are my new employee's training needs?
- How can I meet these needs?
- How can I conduct a training programme to ensure that he acquires the knowledge and skills to help me in the most efficient manner?
- How can I check the effectiveness of the training programme?

The rest of this chapter attempts to answer these questions. The phases of the training process are shown in figure 17. (The figure includes the links between training and company policy to emphasise the necessity for this integration.)

Stage 1. The identification of training needs

'I don't know why I've been sent on this course. I don't see how it can help me in my job.' Such a statement from a participant on a training course indicates that a thorough analysis of training needs has not preceded the decision that training is necessary. The importance of clearly defining needs before embarking on a training programme cannot be over-emphasised.

A training need can be defined as the gap between the requirements for skills and knowledge inherent in the job and those possessed by the current job holder. It is vital that this gap is adequately analysed to establish exactly what training is required. (See figure 18.)

It is misleading to imply that training needs analysis should take place only at the level of the job. A thorough analysis starts with an attempt to assess total organisational training needs in the context of:

- management's plans for the future of the organisation;
- the current organisation structure;
- current expectations about the use of employees.

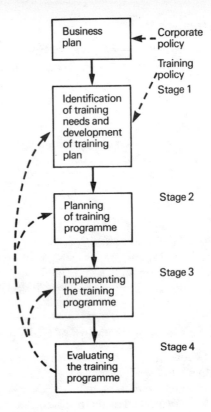

Figure 17. Training process

Figure 18. Training needs analysis

Self-check

Bob Brown owns a bakery. The business has been in existence for over fifty years and has prospered. Capital has accumulated. The firm has a good reputation and there is potential for expansion. The management team consists of Bob, as managing director, and a sales manager. Bob is a trained baker and spends most of his time supervising production. The sales manager supervises the delivery workers, checking van loads in the morning, and returns and cash at the end of the day. From time to time Bob has looked at retail outlets and other possible bakery premises with a view to expansion. However, he seems to lack both the time and the energy to make his dreams of expansion a reality. If you were hired as a consultant, what training needs would you identify for Bob's Bakery?

This is a trick question! The real need is for a change in organisation. We have very scanty information here but a superficial analysis would suggest that the jobs of Bob, in particular, and the sales manager should be redefined to allow them to plan the company's future; they should be released from many of the demands of day-to-day supervision.

Organisational analysis for identification of training needs

An analysis of organisational characteristics and problems is necessary if training is to be adequately linked to business plans. The sort of information required is:

- existing and new product range;
- planned technological developments;
- planned changes to organisation structure;
- planned changes in work methods;
- current and likely future financial position.

It will also be necessary to use manpower information generated as a result of stage 1 of the manpower planning exercise (see Chapter 2, pp. 16–25).

Review

Think back to what you learnt about the first stage of the manpower planning process. List three types of manpower information which should be collected at this stage.

ANSWER

- Characteristics of current employees, by age, sex, grade, etc.
- Data on the utilisation of employees.
- Analysis of labour turnover.

You could have included information about tasks currently being executed from job descriptions. Also, analyses of accident reports, training reports and so on are useful in an organisational analysis of training needs.

This sounds fine, but in practice many training officers or consultants who embark on such a task find that much of the data is incomplete, over-generalised or of doubtful value.

Self-check

Are job descriptions always an accurate picture of the jobs undertaken by employees? List two ways in which they may be deficient.

ANSWER

- They may be out of date.
- Job descriptions are often a statement of what ought to be rather than what is.

It will be necessary to analyse available data and to supplement it by interviews with employees, managers and personnel specialists, and by direct observation of work.

All this information should be compiled into a report which can form the basis of the training plan.

Training plans

The training plan represents the translation of training needs into action.

Suppose that Fred's Food Processing Company loses a number of unfair dismissal cases. Investigation of the facts behind these dismissals reveals that one of the problems was the inadequate handling of problem employees by supervisors, which was compounded by their lack of understanding of employees' legal rights in this area. An entry in the company training plan to cover this might read:

Training need	Estimated benefit	Action	Respons-ibility	Time scale	Budget
handling of disciplinary cases by first-line supervisors	fewer industrial tribunal cases and the company will be likely to win those which arise	plan and run two-day training course for all first-line supervisors	training depart-ment	com-plete within six months	£2,000

The process of training needs analysis at organisational level is summarised in figure 19.

Training needs analysis at individual level

Before training programmes can be organised for individual employees, it is necessary to analyse their jobs for training purposes.

Job analysis In Chapter 3 we examined briefly the process of job analysis in recruitment and selection. Such analysis is relevant for training purposes. However, the emphasis here is on those aspects of the job which make it difficult to learn. It is important to specify what procedures, techniques and skills the trainee must be proficient at by the end of a programme of training. This can be done by means of a job specification.

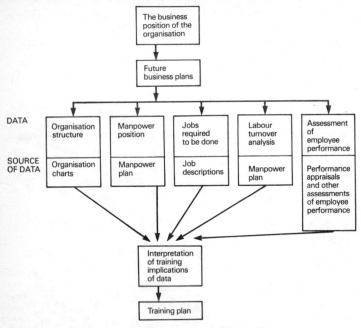

Figure 19. Training needs at organisation level

Review

Look back to the discussion of personnel specifications in Chapter 3, pp. 41–3. Bearing in mind the focus of a job specification required for training purposes, list two headings whichyou would want to use in compiling such a document.

ANSWER

- Knowledge.
- Skills.

In re-examining Chapter 3 you should have noted that many of the headings in a specification of the characteristics of the ideal candidate for recruitment and selection purposes are unsuitable for use in training. This is because they are not amenable to training. Only in the totalitarian world of Big Brother might an employee be 'trained' to have domestic circumstances and interests ideal for the requirements of the job. Thus most specifications used in training needs analysis have the two basic headings listed above. Individual employees' knowledge and skills can then be compared with these and training programmes designed accordingly.

Assessment of individual training needs is one of the outputs of the performance appraisal process (see Chapter 7). Alternative methods of undertaking such an assessment are:

- assessment centres (see Chapter 9); and
- psychological testing (see Chapter 3).

Stage 2. The planning of training programmes

Activity

Earlier in this chapter you were asked to imagine that you were a shop-owner who had recently recruited a school leaver for training. Suppose that you have just completed an analysis of the young person's training needs and are ready to plan a training programme. List four questions which you would need to ask now.

ANSWER

- What are the overall objectives of the training programme?
- Where and when should training take place?
- What should be the content of the training programme?
- What learning methods should be used?

You would also need to know who would undertake the training and who would administer it.

Specification of training objectives

Ideally the objectives of a training programme should be expressed in terms of the behaviour expected of the trainee when training is complete.

‖   *Self-check*

‖   Look at the extract from the training plan for Fred's Food
‖   Processing Company on p. 125. List two possible objectives
‖   for the training programme which will have to be organised
‖   for the supervisors.

By the end of the training programme supervisors should be able
to:

- demonstrate a working knowledge of the law on discipline and
  dismissal;
- demonstrate improved skills in the handling of disciplinary
  interviews.

The objectives of training programmes should fit trainees' needs.
Note that the first objective here is related to supervisors'
needs for knowledge and the second to the skills which they
require in order to interact effectively with those they supervise.

Timing of training programmes

The main considerations are:

- the need to minimise disruption to the trainee's work group;
- the trainee's view of the most appropriate time for training;
- the optimum integration between job demands and the
  content of the training programme – it is not much use to send
  trainees on courses when there will not be any immediate
  opportunity to use newly acquired skills or knowledge;
- the availability of trainers, training rooms and other necessary
  resources;
- the need to work within budgetary constraints.

Location of training programmes

‖   *Self-check*

‖   List three places where the shop-owner's assistant can be
‖   trained.

ANSWER

- Off-the-job training at the place of work.
- On-the-job training at the place of work.
- External training programmes.

Off-the-job training at the workplace Most large organisations have a training centre or training room. The advantage of such 'in-house' provision is that it can encourage identification with the organisation and thus the integration between work and training. Also, if all trainees are fellow employees, cross-fertilisation of ideas and the breaking down of departmental barriers can occur. Possible disadvantages include the exertion of pressure on trainees to return to their jobs if crises arise, thus hampering learning.

On-the-job training at the work-place 'Sitting by Nellie' has long been favoured as a means of passing job knowledge and skills to new employees. Learning can be put into practice straight away. However, the success of this approach depends very much on the quality of 'Nellie', whose bad habits the trainee may acquire or who may be unable to pass on job knowledge.

> *Self-check*
>
> What two steps would you suggest in order to overcome the potential problems of 'sitting by Nellie':

ANSWER

- Ensure that 'Nellie' performs the job exactly in line with management's requirements.
- Train 'Nellie' to be an effective teacher and coach (see Chapter 9, pp. 156–7).

This will not overcome problems of work environment. The hustle and bustle of a busy office may not be conducive to training a typist to be an effective word processor operator.

External courses Sometimes it is not economic to design 'in-house' programmes to meet trainees' needs. In addition development programmes for managers and specialist staff, especially those which lead to formal qualifications, frequently have an educational orientation. Such provision is normally available only externally. The advantages of external courses are:

- the tuition may be better than can be provided within the organisation;
- trainees may feel freer to question and experiment;
- mixing with people from other organisations may facilitate learning. For example, managers may learn that there are other options in the resolution of industrial relations problems by contact with their counterparts in other institutions.

The use of trainers

External trainers or consultants can be used to run training programmes, or the organisation can use suitable employees, usually training specialists. The relevant considerations here are:

- whether the training department or others available as trainers in the organisation have sufficient expertise and time available to undertake the training programme;
- what financial resources are available;
- whether it is desirable to encourage trainees to learn about the relevant policies and practices of other organisations; external trainers are often able to help here.

When external trainers or consultants are used, it is vital to brief them properly with relevant details of the organisation, the training needs analysis on which the programme is to be based, the backgrounds and expectations of the trainees and the training traditions of the organisation.

Administration of training

It does not follow that you can be sure of successful training if you hire the right trainer. Effective administration of the training process is also vital.

Self-check

You are a participant on a one-day course in your organisation. The programme says that coffee will be served in the training room at 10.45 a.m. By 11.00 a.m. it has not arrived. Would such a minor problem impair your learning?

Such errors may appear minor but can impair learning. Good training administrators ensure that:

- clear joining instructions are sent to participants well before the start of the programme;
- trainees understand the objectives of the programme;
- training is uninterrupted and necessary services (training materials, meals, etc.) are available.

Content of training programmes

The basis of our understanding of this subject lies in an area of psychology known as learning theory. Unfortunately, while the learning theorists have provided us with some pointers to the conditions under which training best takes place, they have been unable to find a solution for every case where training is necessary. Different people learn in different ways. Here is some guidance from learning theory which is relevant to the design of training programmes.

- Elements of new knowledge required by trainees must be identified and presented in a way which aids learning.
- Learning is assisted if it can be related to the trainee's previous experience. Trainers should be familiar with the background of trainees and should try to 'speak their language'.
- Learning often occurs through experience. Trainees should be given the opportunity to use previous experience and to practise newly acquired skills and knowledge.
- 'Learning how to learn' is a skill which trainees should be helped to acquire. Thus trainers should be prepared to provide access to assistance with literacy and numeracy as well as generally to facilitate the learning process.
- Trainees' rates and methods of learning vary greatly. Older

people, for example, differ from younger people in this respect.

- Some trainees reach a standstill or plateau in their learning from time to time. Trainers must try to understand the reasons for this to help trainees to make further progress.
- One of the most important influences on trainees' progress is their level of motivation. We looked at motivation theory in Chapter 6. Trainers should be aware of factors likely to affect trainees' motivation.

Self-check

List three characteristics of learner-centred approaches to training.

ANSWER

- The trainee is responsible for his own learning.
- The trainee has the right to analyse his own learning needs.
- The trainee can design his own training programme.

If you adopt this approach to training you see the role of the trainer as facilitator and counsellor rather than as teacher.

Training methods

Activity

Talk to someone involved in training. Ask them to tell you about the training methods they have used. Then list four of the training methods.

Probably your items will be contained in the following list:

- lectures;
- one-to-one instruction;
- conferences;
- workshops;
- case studies;
- roleplay;
- discussions;

- experiential learning;
- sensitivity training;
- action learning;
- brainstorming;
- coaching;
- projects;
- distance learning or self-study.

These categories are not mutually exclusive. For example, experiential learning workshops can be run.

We lack space here to examine the relative merits of each method; however some general comments are relevant. Already in this chapter we have mentioned two categorisations of training methods:

- by location of training; and
- by relationship between trainer and trainee.

Review

List three types of training which are examples of the first categorisation and two examples of the second.

ANSWER

- Off-the-job training at the place of work.
- On-the-job training at the place of work.
- External courses.

And:

- Teacher-centred approaches.
- Learner-centred approaches.

Trainers must select methods which are suitable to the needs of the trainees and to the resources available. It is useful for this to be done in conjunction with trainees after making sure that they understand the aims and objectives of training. 'Variety is the spice of life' in training and a number of methods can usefully be combined. For example, trainers frequently are subject to pressure from line managers to shorten training programmes in the interests of short-term productivity. Trainers can accommodate such pressures sometimes by encouraging trainees to use well-designed self-study texts. Attendance on a training programme can be used for learning in areas where participative methods must be used. However, self study or distance learning is not without its problems for the trainee.

Review

Look back to the guidance from learning theory related to the design of training programmes on pp. 131–2. List three potential problems of self-study materials in aiding trainees' learning.

ANSWER

- The link between the content of such materials and trainees' previous experience may not be readily apparent.
- Trainees may reach learning plateaux and find it difficult to progress.
- Trainees may lack the study skills to cope with the material.

These potential disadvantages may be overcome wholly or in part if the trainee has a coach or mentor in the organisation who is capable of assisting with learning problems. This may be a trainer or a trained manager.

Stage 3. Implementing training programmes

You will have learnt by now that effective training programmes depend on thorough training needs analysis and good programme planning and design. However, if the delivery of the programme is inadequate, this preparatory work will have been wasted.

Selection of appropriate trainees for training

Some points to bear in mind here are:

- **Size of the group** Some participative methods such as roleplay cannot be conducted effectively with large numbers. Even with more teacher-centred methods large numbers may be unhelpful; trainees can fail to become actively involved in their own learning.

- **Mix of participants** Work group members may be assisted to work together more effectively by a common training experience such as a team-building workshop. Conversely individuals may develop ideas about possible new ways of solving work problems from a training programme which gives the opportunity to meet people from other departments or organisations.
- **The process of selecting trainees should also involve their superiors** Much useful learning from training programmes fails to be carried back into the workplace. If the trainee's supervisor is responsible for pre- and post-programme briefing, this is less likely to occur.
- **Trainees should want to be trained** Only those employees who wish to undergo training should do so. Sometimes trainers have to work with course participants who have been told that they must be trained. In these cases there is resistance to learning and little is achieved.

Conducting training programmes in accordance with objectives and design

We stressed the need to give care to the selection of trainers and training administrators, when we examined the planning of training programmes. Effective communication with trainees is vital, as is the careful organisation of materials and other resources.

Give trainees feedback on performance during the training programme

Informing trainees of their progress during training encourages appropriate behaviour to be continued and inappropriate behaviour to be dropped. It allows the trainer to discover whether trainees have learning problems and to help these to be overcome.

Stage 4. The evaluation of training programmes

Evaluation methods

Post-programme evaluation Most trainers will tell you that the best time to get a positive reaction to a training programme from trainees is at the end of the last day. This reaction may not be valid in that the trainee is often in a state of euphoria at this time with lots of ideas buzzing around in his head. It may be appropriate to administer a questionnaire at the end of the course which is clearly linked with the training which has been undertaken. It can be linked to a pre-course questionnaire to check the degree to which the course has come up to the trainee's expectations and has increased his knowledge.

Because of the problems of administering such questionnaires at the end of a course, some trainers send them to participants weeks or months afterwards. This too has its disadvantages in that the response rate tends to be low.

Self-check

What is the greatest validity problem of post-course reaction questionnaires completed by trainees?

To be effective, evaluation must measure whether training objectives have been achieved; that is, whether the trainee's job performance has improved. Asking for trainees' reactions to a course or even attempting to measure improvements in their knowledge does not assess whether they are more effective employees as a result of training.

Other training evaluation methods

Activity

Talk again to the trainer you questioned about training methods. Ask how the results of training are evaluated other than by trainees' reactions to it.

Your trainer may have found this question difficult to answer honestly! Training is rarely evaluated other than via trainees' reactions. However, it can be evaluated with reference to:

- the behaviour of the individual employee on the job;
- organisational performance in areas where training has been undertaken;
- the degree to which the whole organisation has benefited from training and development.

What is certain is that the further away you get from trainees' reactions to training the more difficult evaluation becomes. This is because other factors may be responsible for the changes detected.

Self-check

Fred's Food Processing Company sends all its supervisors on the training programme outlined in the extract from the training plan on p. 125. The following year, claims of unfair dismissal fall by 50 per cent and the company wins all the cases which go to industrial tribunal. Can it be claimed that this is the result of the training programme?

It might be. Alternatively it could be that rising unemployment has made dismissed employees more reluctant to take up cases for fear of being labelled as potential troublemakers by possible new employers. Or the company's increased success rate in tribunal cases could be due to the increased quality of its representation.

Self-check

Who other than trainees should be asked to contribute to the evaluation of training programmes?

ANSWER

- Trainers.
- Trainees' managers.

Evaluating changes in trainees' job behaviour

Managers can be consulted and trainees and trainers can meet in workshops or with individual managers to discuss the effects of training. It is best if this occurs some months after the completion of training so that the full effects can be evaluated. This can act as useful reinforcement for the trainee and can assist trainers to make decisions about modifications to training programmes.

Another useful mechanism is for trainees to be encouraged to compile action plans at the end of a training programme. The success of the training programme can be evaluated by the degree to which the plan is achieved.

Evaluation by trainers of their contribution

It is important that trainers systematically review the extent to which they assisted trainees to meet the objectives of a training programme.

Evaluation at organisational level

Relevant indicators include:

- labour tutnover rates;
- accident rates;
- waste of materials;
- absenteeism;
- productivity.

Only thorough investigation is likely to reveal whether improvements in these areas can be attributed to training. Some organisations use a training committee of senior managers to supervise such an assessment.

Feedback of evaluation results

To complete the systematic approach to training outlined at the beginning of this chapter, it is vital to feed back the results of evaluation to all those involved in the training process.

Self-check

List three reasons for evaluating training programmes.

ANSWER

- To enable the effectiveness of investment in training to be appraised.
- To provide feedback about trainees' performance which can be used in subsequent training.
- To improve future training programmes.

Role of the training specialist

In Chapter 1 we categorised the roles of personnel specialists as:

- audit;
- executive;
- facilitator;
- consultancy;
- service.

> *Review*
>
> Give an example of an activity undertaken by a training specialist under each of these headings.

ANSWERS

Audit Checking that job descriptions are accurate prior to embarking on a training needs analysis.

Executive Running a training course.

Facilitator Assisting trainees to identify their learning needs and objectives.

Consultancy Advising a manager on the degree to which training can resolve a problem of inadequate employee performance.

Service Providing management with regular reports on training activities which have taken place in the organisation.

9 | Developing people for the future

Here our focus is the often lengthy training and development programmes for the career development of employees.

Self-check

> Name two categories of employees for whom long-term career development programmes are often undertaken.

The most obvious category is those with supervisory or managerial potential and graduate trainees. Female workers or members of ethnic minority groups may be selected for development as part of the implementation of equal opportunities policies.

In this chapter we shall examine each of these areas in turn. The subject of management development is covered in the greatest depth for two reasons: firstly, because almost all organisations attempt to develop potential managers and, secondly, because the principles involved here can be applied to other categories of staff. By the end of the chapter you should be able to apply a systematic approach to the development of employees thought capable of progressing to more responsible jobs.

Management development

In the postwar period there has been a great increase in both the time and money devoted to management development by employers in this country.

Self-check

> List three reasons for this.

ANSWER

• Increased competition from foreign companies has prompted

many employers to search for ways of improving productivity. It has been recognised that a major factor in achieving this is the calibre of management.

- As some organisations recognised the value of developing effective managers for the reason suggested above, so others have accepted that 'what's sauce for the goose is sauce for the gander'.

- The manager's job has generally become more difficult during this period. Hence it has become more important that he is adequately trained to cope with such things as: (i) more complex decision-making because of the increased size of the organisation in which he works; (ii) the growth of specialisms in managerial techniques and hence the need to interact effectively with marketing, finance and personnel specialists or to understand in some depth available knowledge in each field; (iii) the effects of labour shortages and, latterly, of surpluses (though shortages of skilled workers still exist in many industries); (iv) the increased unionisation of much of the labour force; (v) the increasingly instrumental attitude to work of many employees; (vi) the impact of employment legislation on employees' rights at work.

These are not the only reasons. For example, you may have mentioned the growth in the application of the social sciences to management in the hope that here may lie some new solutions to management's productivity problems. In addition the state has encouraged management development initiatives by grants from industrial training boards and more recently the Manpower Services Commission. The number of people undertaking undergraduate and postgraduate management courses has increased greatly during the postwar period. This seems to have encouraged those in managerial roles to seek exposure to similar development programmes.

The focus of management development

Prescriptions for the development of effective managers vary greatly. It is superficially simple to implement a 'package' for the off-the-job training of potential managers. It is less easy to develop techniques which match the needs of the particular organisation. Nevertheless it has now largely been accepted that the latter approach is more likely to be successful.

> ### Self-check
>
> 'Successful managers share a number of characteristics.' Would you agree that a statement such as this could be used to justify the design of training programmes helpful to the development of all managers?

If you agree with the view that management development should be geared to the particular organisational circumstances of the manager's job, your answer to the question will have been in the negative. The requirements for effective management will differ greatly from organisation to organisation depending on the nature of the market for products and labour, the size of the organisation, its history and so on.

A systematic approach to manager development

You would be well advised to analyse managerial jobs before attempting to select and develop those capable of filling them.

> ### Review
>
> You are charged with responsibility for the process of management development in your organisation. Think back to Chapter 2, 'Planning for people', and to the last chapter on training; then list the questions which you would need to ask yourself to develop a systematic process for the selection and development of people with potential for managerial positions within five years.

ANSWER

- What managerial jobs will we need to fill in five years' time?
- What will be the characteristics (knowledge, skills and personal qualities) of the individuals suitable to fill these positions?
- How can we select some people for development to these positions?

- What training needs do these people have?
- What development programmes can we plan and implement to meet these needs?
- How can we evaluate the process?

The rest of the discussion of management development in this chapter attempts to answer these questions.

The link with manpower planning

As the first of the questions listed above implies, we need to estimate the demand for managers in five years' time and the likely supply.

> *Review*
>
> List three facts which you would need to know in order to forecast the *supply* of managers in an organisation in five years' time. (You will remember that we covered manpower supply planning in Chapter 2.)

ANSWER

- Number in managerial jobs now – by grade, age, job, etc.
- Retirements over the next five years.
- Labour turnover over the next five years.

You may also have mentioned movement into other jobs as a result of promotion, demotion or other job changes.

You should not have listed any factor associated with changes in the nature of the business over the next five years – expansion or contraction, for example. This must be taken into account as part of manpower demand planning, which is also vital in attempting to estimate the number of managers required by the organisation in five years' time.

> *Review*
>
> Having estimated the demand for managers in five years' time and the likely supply, list the next three stages of the manpower planning process.

ANSWER

- An examination of the degree to which the manpower supply forecast and the manpower demand forecast match.
- An identification of critical shortages or surpluses of labour.
- An evaluation of the options for coping with any mismatch between supply and demand.

Very often it is decided that, if the organisation is likely to have a shortage of managers in the future, the gap should be filled by the development and promotion of existing employees.

|| *Self-check*
|| Give two reasons for this.

ANSWERS

- As we have seen, the characteristics of managerial effectiveness often seem to depend on the particular nature of the organisation. Hence employees who 'know the ropes' may be a safer bet than outsiders.
- The opportunity of promotion to a managerial position may act as a spur to hard work.

Other factors may be the uncertainty and the cost of the recruitment and selection process – 'better the devil you know . . .'! Information from performance appraisal and personnel records should act as a basis for such judgements of existing employees. Early identification of potential gives time for systematic development prior to promotion.

Conversely, senior management in particular are often externally recruited because an injection of 'new blood' can help ward off stagnation and complacency. There are no easy prescriptions for success in personnel management. Choice of a strategy should be made after a careful consideration of organisational circumstances.

Managerial succession planning

To ensure that replacements will be available for managers who leave or retire, and that suitable people are ready to fill newly created managerial positions, managerial succession planning is undertaken in many organisations. This involves the recording of information from manpower planning and assessments of performance and potential in such a way as to facilitate decision-making on promotions and the development of those earmarked as having potential.

Self-check

Figure 20 is an example of a succession chart. Examine it carefully. Then answer the following questions.

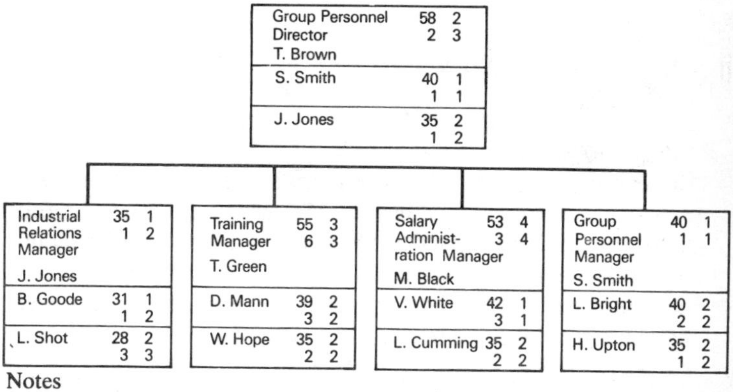

Figure 20. Succession chart for senior personnel specialists.

Notes

Each position on this organisation chart is shown with the name of the present incumbent and that of a short- and a long-term successor. Each name is followed by four numbers:

1. The number in the top left-hand corner indicates age of employee.

2. The number in the bottom left-hand corner indicates highest qualification of employee:
   1. higher degree;
   2. first degree;
   3. professional qualification;
   4. national diploma;
   5. national certificate;
   6. other.

3. The number in the top right-hand corner indicates performance in the current job assessed on a five-point scale:
   1. excellent;
   2. very good;
   3. adequate;
   4. barely adequate;
   5. inadequate;

4. The number in the bottom right-hand corner indicates promotability on a four-point scale;
   1. ready for promotion;
   2. promotion with development;
   3. probably not promotable;
   4. should be transferred.

1 How old is the group personnel director?
2 Which of his subordinates should be transferred to other, presumably less responsible, work?
3 How would the group personnel manager feel if he were told that he is the personnel director's immediate successor.
4 List three potential problems in using this chart.

ANSWERS

1 58.
2 M. Black, the salary administration manager.
3 Initially he would feel very pleased but if promotion did not take place relatively quickly he probably would become disillusioned.
4 Firstly the chart is rather complex. Unless the organisation is a large bureaucracy, it ought to be possible to record the information more simply. Secondly, care is needed in the use of rating scales for the assessment of performance and potential (see Chapter 7, pp 110–11). Thirdly, it is difficult to decide how much of the information contained in succession charts should be communicated to the employees concerned. You should have been stimulated to think about this by question 3. At one extreme, if the entire chart is devised by the most senior executive and locked away, its value will be very limited. On the other hand, if relevant information is communicated to all employees named on the chart, those thought incapable of further promotion may become demotivated whilst those earmarked for career progression, such as the group personnel manager, may become frustrated if opportunities fail to materialise.

Succession planning is vital if the continuity of the business is to be maintained without hitches when key managerial positions become vacant. The lessons for successful planning are:

● keep it simple;
● back up succession plans with current personnel records which include details of training received and job performance;
● try to make the process as informal as possible.

Analysis of training needs

In the last chapter we looked generally at the process of establishing training needs both at organisational and individual level.

Review

List five types of information needed to analyse training needs at organisational level.

ANSWER

- the structure of the organisation;
- the manpower position;
- the jobs required to be done;
- an analysis of labour turnover;
- an assessment of employee performance.

Before selecting candidates for management development, job analysis should have been undertaken and job specifications for training purposes drawn up to identify the skills and knowledge required. It will also be necessary to use the personnel specification drawn up for recruitment and selection purposes as a guide to the personal qualities of potential managers.

Selecting for management development

Self-check

List two possible methods of identifying candidates for development as tomorrow's managers.

ANSWER

- Performance appraisal interviews and records.
- Systematic selection methods.

Performance appraisal

Review

List three possible advantages of attempting to assess potential during a performance appraisal interview.

ANSWER

- Employees can be given feedback on their performance as part of career counselling.
- Manager and employee together can assess the latter's training and development needs, if career goals are to be achieved.
- This is a relatively cheap method of assessing potential as compared with assessment centres, for example (see p. 149).

However, you also should be aware that many managers lack knowledge of career paths and find it difficult to discuss career development with their subordinates. Also the appraisee's immediate boss is likely to be familiar only with performance in the current job. This may be an inadequate indicator of the ability to do other jobs.

Designing selection systems to identify potential

Review

Bearing in mind the discussion of the selection interview in Chapter 3, list three disadvantages of using an interview as the sole method of selecting employees for management development.

ANSWER

- Selection interviews may be only as reliable as sticking pins in a list as a method of selecting the best candidate.
- Interviewers may be affected by the 'halo effect' or other types of bias. In selecting a successor, a manager may select 'in his own image'.
- As a result, interviewers may ask faulty questions or fail to listen adequately to candidates' answers.

Assessment centres

The 'acid test' of an employee's capability to become a manager is the ability to do the job. Assessment centres have been developed as an attempt to simulate all or part of the job and to observe candidates' reactions to it. The origins of assessment centres lie in the War Office selection boards developed during the Second World War because of the need to select soldiers from the ranks for officer training.

The term 'assessment centre' is generally used to cover the assessment of a group of individuals by a team of judges using a comprehensive and integrated series of techniques, such as psychological tests, interviews and simulation exercises. A major use is the selection of employees for development.

Typically an assessment centre consists of:

- A leaderless group exercise in which candidates are given a group task to undertake in a given time, for example the planning of a conference or the relocation of a factory. Assessors sit outside the group making notes on participants' behaviour. Attributes for assessment include assertiveness, influence and leadership. Sometimes this activity takes the form of a business game in which participants in teams must operate at a profit in a given market. Sometimes teams compete.
- A report-writing exercise in which participants, again under time pressure, write a report on their own jobs or on some other aspect of the business. Characteristics assessed include written communication skills, breadth of understanding and logical development of ideas.
- An in-tray exercise consisting of a sample of problems which a manager might find on his desk on a bad day. The aim is to test the ability to work under pressure, to delegate and to analyse and solve problems.

Other common elements of assessment centres include oral presentations, interviews and psychological tests of ability and personality.

Self-check

How would you decide what activities to include in an assessment centre?

In answering this you should have taken into account:

- the characteristics of the job for which participants are being selected;
- the size of budget to run the assessment centre;
- the number of trained assessors available.

Characteristics tested during assessment centres

A detailed and accurate personnel specification is an essential prerequisite of an assessment centre. The activities to be included should be designed to test the characteristics of the ideal candidate laid down in this specification. For example, it would be futile to include an oral presentation if such a skill is not a requirement of the job. Where candidates are being chosen for development rather than immediate promotion, it will be necessary to take account of this in selecting dimensions for assessment. Frequently, as we saw above, activities can be chosen which test more than one dimension.

The cost of assessment centres

Assessment centres are not worth doing unless done well. The costs involved include the time of those who design and run the centre as well as those who train the assessors. These can be considerable since assessment centres usually last from two days to a week and involve one assessor for every two or three candidates. In addition external consultants are frequently hired to design and oversee the process.

Assessor training

Assessors are usually senior managers.

‖ *Self-check*

List three attributes of effective assessors.

They should be:

- familiar with the jobs for development to which candidates are being considered;
- committed to management development and to the use of assessment centres as part of this;
- prepared to give sufficient time both to training as assessors and to involvement in assessment centres.

Training is vital. Managers do not generally possess the skills of recording and reporting verbal and non-verbal behaviour. In addition they must develop common definitions of assessment dimensions and of associated rating scales. Training usually involves assessors doing the exercises as assessees and discussing ratings. They also may observe assessment centres.

Feedback to participants

At the end of the assessment centre, assessors pool their judgements. The centre may be used simply to accept or reject candidates. More often it is a basis for the counselling of participants as an aid to the planning of their career development.

Reliability and validity of assessment centres

Research indicates that assessment centres, if well designed and well run, are better predictors of future job performance than interviews alone. Though they are more expensive than appraisal interviews, the extra cost should result in more accurate predictions of potential. The counselling which follows a good assessment centre should be a sound basis on which to build subsequent management development.

Designing management development programmes

The nature of the gap between the characteristics of the potential manager and the requirements of the job it will be necessary for him to do in the future should be delineated as a result of an assessment centre or through performance appraisal interview. A programme of development must then be designed. There are large numbers of management development techniques but, as we said earlier in the chapter, these must be appropriate to organisational and individual circumstances.

Activity

Talk to two managers about how they learnt to do their jobs. List the four items which they mentioned most frequently.

Probably the most likely categories were:

- doing the job;
- doing other jobs;
- training courses at the place of work or elsewhere;
- education programmes such as post-experience management courses.

Other sources of learning for managers or potential managers include:

- life experience;
- radio, television and newspapers;
- friends, relatives or other influential people in life;
- thinking, introspection or self-assessment;
- pre-experience courses, such as business studies degrees or national diplomas.

We see from this list that management development can be teacher-centred or learner-centred in the sense that it builds on the individual's own experiences.

Teacher-centred approaches

Most managers have experienced some sort of taught management course. The distinction between education and training made in the last chapter is relevant here. Managers need specific skills and knowledge to be effective. Training courses are designed to teach selling techniques, particular areas of legislation, negotiating skills, effective speaking and so on. If well designed and run, these are useful, especially if they give the opportunity for participants to exchange views and experiences with others in similar positions.

Management education specialists argue that managers or potential specialists must be flexible and adaptable to meet the changing circumstances of business organisations. They must be aware of the environmental context – political, social and economic – and able to resolve problems and meet new situations. A variety of diploma and higher degree courses have been developed to this end by universities, polytechnics and other institutions. Their quality varies greatly and the intending user should carefully scrutinise a programme of his choice prior to enrolment.

Self-check

Some managers expect teachers of management education and training programmes to be the fount of all wisdom. Is this realistic?

No. A key skill of the management teacher is to help participants to learn from each other as well as from lectures and the other resources of the providing institution.

Learner-centred approaches: encouraging managers to learn from experience

Whilst good management teachers will assist managers to build positively on their experience, programme content and teaching methods are largely prescribed. There are other approaches to management development which focus on the needs of the learner.

In the last chapter we outlined the main characteristics of learner-centred approaches to training.

Review

List three of these characteristics.

ANSWER

- The learner is in charge of his own learning rather than dependent on a teacher.
- The learner initiates his own learning process and thus may analyse his own learning needs, define his own objectives and so on.
- The learner can choose what to learn and at what pace.

Learner-centred approaches to management development are now well established. Here we examine two of them – action learning and self-managed learning.

Action learning This approach is based on the work of Reg Revans who, after an industrial career, became a professor of management. He quickly became disenchanted with management education, saying quite simply, 'Courses won't work. We must give management education back to the managers and let them learn with and from each other during real work.'

Thus action learning programmes have two common elements:

- participating managers work on complex and important problems to which the final answer is not known but to which a series of acceptable next moves might be suggested;
- these managers meet together regularly and on equal terms in 'sets' to report to each other and to discuss problems and progress.

Programmes vary in their structure but participants spend either all or part of their working time on the diagnosis of a complex and important business problem. The important difference between this and other management development or research projects is that participation in action learning means that managers must 'own' the problem and must be able to implement their solutions.

Revans favours the exchange of participants between organisations, so that a manager experienced in one organisational context is placed in a strange environment with a complex problem. In this way there is a freshness of approach and a likelihood that organisational conventions will be broken.

A vital element of action learning programmes is 'sets' of four to six participants. These meet regularly and are assisted by a set adviser. The function of the set is to help participants resolve the business problem which each owns. The set adviser, who may be a teacher, trainer, consultant, personnel specialist or manager, helps set members in a mutual process of giving and receiving help and generally assists with the action learning process.

Self-check

Which of the roles played by personnel specialists, described at the end of Chapter 1, does this description of the functions of the set adviser most closely resemble?

ANSWER

The *facilitator* role in the sense that the adviser helps participants to resolve the problems which are the focus of action learning, assists them to support each other in these tasks and to learn about the process of learning and the role of the set in this.

Self-check

List three differences between action learning and more conventional management education programmes with a defined syllabus, where participants are more dependent on teachers.

ANSWER

- An assumption of action learning is that managers learn by managing, whereas more conventional management education programmes aim to teach managers to manage.
- Participants on action learning programmes 'own' a real business problem and are responsible for implementing a solution.
- The role of staff on action learning programmes is to provide

the conditions in which managers can learn by resolving practical problems. By contrast teachers on more conventional programmes are concerned with the transfer of knowledge and skills to participants within the limits of a predetermined syllabus.

Self-managed learning There are many similarities between this approach and action learning; participants in both programmes are responsible for the management of their own learning and there is no predetermined curriculum. Self-managed learning programmes also use 'sets' as a support and progress mechanism.

However, in self-managed learning programmes, managers are completely free to analyse their own learning needs and to choose the associated learning methods in conjunction with set members and staff associated with the programme. The resultant individual programme of study need not be centred on a business problem as in action learning. Rather the manager sets his learning objectives in the context of himself and his career objectives. His task is to fulfil the requirements of his individually defined course of study. In doing this he may use a variety of learning methods such as attendance at lectures, projects in his own or another organisation, roleplays or guided reading.

Management coaching

Coaching rests on the assumption that someone who has performed a job is qualified to teach a subordinate who aspires to positions of greater responsibility. To be an effective coach the manager must help the subordinate to identify his development needs and agree with him how development can best take place. The coach should hold regular sessions with the subordinate to review progress and to give further counselling and guidance.

A major advantage of coaching as part of a management development programme, which also may include courses and other more formal learning experiences, is that a close relationship between superior and subordinate should ease problems of integrating new learning with the requirements of present or future jobs.

A word of caution must be sounded! Not all managers are effective coaches. Training in relevant skills is vital, as are certain personal qualities.

Activity

Try to analyse your own development needs in your job. If you can take your list to your boss and ask him to help you, prepare a personal development plan.

This should be a useful exercise in itself but for our purposes here, after the interview, you should list four qualities or skills which your boss needed in order to help you.

ANSWER

- Good communication skills.
- Willingness to listen and to learn.
- A participative style rather than a desire to impose solutions on you.
- Interest in you and in your development.

Evaluation of management development

It is probably more important to review the results of management development systematically than for other types of training activity. This is because the expenditure per employee of both time and money is likely to be greater.

Review

List three ways of evaluating the results of management development. Think back to our discussion of the evaluation of training in the last chapter, pp. 136–8, to help you to do this.

ANSWER

- Evaluating management development activities such as courses.
- Evaluating the performance of participants on the job.

- Evaluating the performance of the manager's department or section.

In deciding on your answers to this question you should have recalled the problems of evaluating the results of training discussed in the last chapter. Only by a continuous process of feedback can management development activities become closely aligned to organisational needs.

Career development for young people

After our examination of management development we will look briefly at planned development activities for young entrants to organisations. These are usually eighteen-year-old school leavers or graduates. Generally, approaches to their development are of two types:

- the 'Cook's tour' of the organisation;
- specific training in one job.

Activity

When I first graduated I went to work as a personnel management trainee at the headquarters of a large retailing and wholesaling organisation. The selection process was intensive and highly competitive, bearing considerable resemblence to an assessment centre in the techniques employed. I was keen to gain experience of personnel management. The personnel department was divided into sections dealing with recruitment and selection, industrial relations, salary administration, employee benefits and so on. Trainees were given a 'Cook's tour' of the department, spending three months in each section.

Initially we were enthusiastic about this, believing that it would afford the opportunity to acquire a good grounding in all the aspects of personnel work. I became disillusioned after weeks in the 'sickness section' dealing with the administration of the company's scheme under the supervision of a clerk the same age as myself whose experience of personnel management was limited to his present job. I spent my days doing manual calculations of sickness entitlements and benefits. I never saw an employee or a manager. My next move was to the industrial relations section. Here the work was more interesting and I was supervised by a graduate industrial relations officer who was keen to help me to learn. To cope with the job I needed considerable understanding both of industrial relations and of payment-by-results systems, since the task was to prepare negotiating briefs for management. I tried to gain appropriate knowledge by intensive reading of files of previous cases. This was not entirely satisfactory since my learning was very fragmented and needed consolidation.

The industrial relations officer was frequently out at factories assisting with negotiations, and his superior, the industrial relations manager, was openly hostile to me. He had opposed the appointment of graduate trainees, believing that we were a hindrance to the smooth running of the department. We had day-release one day each week to attend a local college course which led to the examinations of the Institute of Personnel Management. The course seemed to have little relevance to our work and we generally saw it as a day off work!

List five problems of career development using a 'Cook's tour' illustrated by this case study.

ANSWER

- The high expectations of the trainees generated by the rigorous nature of the selection process were not fulfilled by the development programme.
- The employees charged with the day-to-day supervision of the trainees were inadequately integrated into the programme. Hence supervision was generally inadequate.
- The development programme was actively opposed by some members of the department.
- There was a failure to ensure that trainees had adequate skills and knowledge to cope with the tasks which they were given or readily available support and guidance when necessary.
- The college course was not integrated with work experience even in the broadest sense.

Only if these problems had been overcome would we have reaped the advantages of such a 'Cook's tour'; that is, we would have learnt about the various types of personnel work and their relationships with each other and with the other parts of the business. A further advantage of such approaches to the development of young people is that they enable them to make better decisions about their career goals. In particular they allow general management trainees to decide on the function of management in which they wish to specialise.

Many young people move straight into a permanent job and receive development related to that job. The advantage of this approach is that it gives greater opportunities for the development of skills, by contrast to the 'tour' which may give trainees a wide but superficial knowledge of the organisation. Young people in junior management, technical or professional roles learn by coping with the demands of their own job rather than by watching others. In this situation a sympathetic boss is vital and, if he is trained as a coach, so much the better.

Equal opportunities in career development

As we shall see in Chapter 11, positive action can be taken to train women or members of ethnic minority groups where it can be shown that they are under-represented in particular jobs. As yet relatively few organisations have taken advantage of these legislative provisions and research has indicated that fear of resentment from other workers is a major factor. However, recently, prompted by community pressure groups, some local authorities and other public bodies have begun to implement equal opportunities policies. As a result programmes to provide development opportunities for members of groups previously under-represented in particular occupations or at certain levels in the organisation, have been started.

Very often targets are established for numbers of women or members of ethnic minorities to be in particular posts within a certain time. This is the manpower planning stage of the development programme. People with the potential to fill the positions in question must then be selected.

Review

Remembering our discussion of a systematic approach to training in the last chapter, and that of management development in this chapter, list the next two stages of an equal opportunities career development programme.

ANSWER

- Analysis of the training needs of those selected for career development, taking into account the gap between the requirements of the jobs they will fill at the end of the development programme and the knowledge and skills which they currently possess.
- The design of an appropriate development programme.

Employees selected for development in this way will have occupied relatively routine jobs for many years, which may not have made full use of their personal capabilities. Hence, equal opportunities programmes usefully include confidence-building activities and assertiveness training as well as very good facilities for counselling and guidance. The support of managers and other people involved in the programme is vital. Some organisations run training programmes in racism and sexism awareness for managers involved in making development and promotion decisions, to help to ensure that career development for members of minority groups becomes a reality as part of the implementation of equal opportunities policies.

A final word on development

People are the organisation's greatest resources for the future:

A wise counsellor was asked, 'If you had to use a single guide for selecting managers, what would it be?' He replied, 'Tell me what the person does if he wakes up shivering in the middle of the night. If he merely covers his head and hopes the cold will go away, I don't want him. If he climbs out of bed into the cold room and gets another blanket, he has potential.' . . . We face a similar choice when thinking about managers for the year 2000. We can rely on present practice and hope to get by, or we can treat the pressures ahead as a challenge and devise ways to harness them.*

Managers for the year 2000, edited by William H. Newman, Prentice Hall, 1978.

I hope that in this chapter I have convinced you that systematic development not only of managers but also of other groups of employees is vital if such future challenges are to be met!

10 | Looking after employees – welfare and counselling services

The development of welfare services in industrial organisations began in the UK in the late nineteenth century, when there was no welfare state and working conditions could be appalling. Some paternalistic employers, most of them Quakers, believed that they had a responsibility to look after their employees for both social and economic reasons. The question we attempt to answer in this chapter is whether it is still necessary for employers to provide welfare services.

Self-check

List two reasons for the provision of welfare services for employees by management.

ANSWER

- To ensure that employees' productive capacity is not handicapped by personal problems.
- To fill gaps in the provision of state welfare services for employed people.

You may also have listed other reasons such as:

- The social responsibilities of employers.
- The legal responsibilities of employers. The law requires employers to provide adequate lighting, fume extraction, air conditioning, facilities for washing, rest breaks and meals and so on. As we shall see in the next chapter the law also lays down statutory minima for the provision of certain rights. Maternity pay and maternity leave would fall into this category.
- The desire to be perceived as a good employer as an aid to recruitment.

It is difficult to prove a link between the provision of welfare services and productivity, but many managers would argue that encouraging employees to have a positive attachment both to their jobs and to the employing organisation is in the interests of economic efficiency. State welfare services are geared to the needs of those who do not work and increasing unemployment has put strains on these.

How can we define 'welfare' in the context of modern personnel management?

The first comprehensive list of the range of personnel management activities to be compiled in Britain was published in 1943.* It listed welfare or employee services activities as:

- Administration of canteen policy.
- Sick club and benevolent and savings schemes.
- Long-service grants.
- Pension and superannuation funds or leaving grants.
- Granting of loans.
- Legal aid.
- Advice on individual problems.
- Assistance to employees in transport, housing, billeting, shopping and other problems.
- Provision of social and recreation facilities.

The comprehensive nature of this list was more an expression of hope for the future than of reality in most organisations in the immediate postwar period. Can it then be said to be some sort of indication of the welfare services provided by employers in the 1980s?

> *Activity*
>
> List the welfare services provided by your employer or, if you are not working, by an organisation known to you.

Most large employers do provide specialist welfare services to

*G.R. Moxon, *Functions of a Personnel Department*, Institute of Personnel Management, 1943.

employees of the sort listed above, though there has been some shift of emphasis from those where state services are now more comprehensive (housing, transport and recreational provision) towards greater provision of counselling and other personal advice services.

Logically it would be expected that the relative absence of labour shortages in a recession would lead to a decline in the provision of welfare services. Such evidence as there is suggests that this may not be occurring. With technological change, more of the organisation's resources tend to be invested in plant and machinery. Hence payments to employees become a lesser proportion of overall operating costs, and so the provision of, for example, counselling services becomes relatively cheap. As the ratio of capital invested per employee increases, management may become more aware of the need for employees to be fully effective. Welfare services are both cheap and efficient to provide.

Self-check

List three reasons why management should not provide welfare services for employees in the 1980s.

ANSWER

- State welfare provision is much more wide-ranging than before, and there is no need for employers to duplicate such services.
- 'Welfare' sounds like nineteenth-century paternalism and 'do-gooding'. It may even be a device for discouraging employees from joining trade unions.
- The provision of such services by employers can increase the gap between the 'haves' and the 'have-nots' in our society, and as such is undesirable.

This is a summary of the counter-arguments to those mounted in favour of welfare provision by employers at the beginning of this chapter. There is no right or wrong answer. Much depends both on your values and on the circumstances of the employing organisation. Some employers have a policy of peaceful competition with trade unions. This usually involves employment policies which are generous by comparison with others. Such employers would tend to provide a full and attractive range of employee welfare services.

Personal services for employees – counselling

Most organisations seem to provide employees with counselling and advice services.

> *Activity*
>
> Give two examples of times when your employer has provided you with advice or counselling. If you are not working at present, ask someone who is working to provide you with the examples.

- Career development.
- Legal advice.
- Housing.
- Bereavement.
- Sickness.
- Domestic problems.
- Retirement.
- Redundancy.
- Working relationships.

You may have had difficulty with this activity, if your organisation does not provide such services formally. Managers or personnel specialists may be called on to help employees in this way but they cannot be called professional counsellors. Few professional counsellors work in the employment field in the UK as compared with the United States.

Who should undertake employee counselling?

The relationship between manager and subordinate often will not be amenable to the development of a counselling relationship. The manager may be concerned with his own status and thus unwilling to put himself into the subordinate's shoes. Also there may be a tendency to be protective of information, which might be useful, such as the employee's *real* prospects of promotion. The employee is likely to find it difficult to seek counselling from his boss. For example, disclosure of domestic problems may hamper promotion prospects.

Specialist personnel staff often take on a counselling role. They may experience fewer problems than line managers. Nevertheless the problems of trust and fear of confidentiality so far as employees are concerned will arise. For this reason, some organisations use specialist independent services staffed by professional counsellors. Even where this is done it is certain that both managers and personnel specialists will take on the role of counsellor from time to time. In order to carry this out effectively they must be trained.

We have stressed the need for professional individual counselling services, but sometimes non-professional helpers may play a very useful role. For example, in career planning, employees can assist each other to identify career and life goals and to plan ways of achieving these. In this way mutual support is possible. This has been found particularly helpful for female employees and members of ethnic minority groups who often fail to achieve their full potential through lack of confidence and skills and a tendency by employers and others to undervalue their abilities. A few employers encourage such counselling as part of equal opportunities programmes.

The skills of counselling

It seems that effective counsellors:

- encourage trust from their clients;
- relate to their clients;
- are people- rather than task-centred;
- encourage clients to clarify the situation and to search for their own solutions rather than depending on others;
- supply relevant information but refrain from giving advice.

For which employees may personal welfare services be necessary?

Young employees Trainees, and employees who have recently completed full-time education, may need special support during the first weeks and months of their employment. Frequently this is provided by those responsible for operating training programmes. Where young people have had to leave home to take a job, employers sometimes provide help with housing.

Those nearing retirement Many employers have encouraged workers nearing retirement age to retire early as part of a policy to reduce the size of the labour force. For these people and those due to retire at the normal date, it is now common practice to provide retirement counselling and / or pre-retirement courses.

> ### *Self-check*
> List three topics which could usefully form part of a pre-retirement course.

ANSWER

- Investment.
- Keeping healthy.
- Activities outside the home.

Other topics which you might have listed are:

- State benefits for retired people.
- Taxation.

Some organisations also provide assistance to retired employees who suffer financial hardship or have personal problems.

Redundant employees Redundancy usually comes as a shock to employees. Hence many employers provide similar support to that provided to those nearing retirement.

> ### *Self-check*
> List four other topics, apart from those included above,

|| which would usefully form part of a course for employees about to become redundant.

ANSWER

- Career counselling.
- Job-search skills.
- Starting your own business.
- Government training schemes.

Frequently at a time of redundancy attention is focused on those who will have to leave, both in terms of the financial compensation for loss of jobs to be awarded and other support services available. Those who will continue as employees should not be forgotten. Often they will have uncertainties about the future of the organisation and their own future within it. Management may need to be particularly vigilant to allay such uncertainties.

The bereaved and the sick Both employees whose close relatives die and those who experience long periods of absence from work because of personal sickness will have financial problems. Personal welfare services can provide advice and assistance.

Group services for employees

Some employee services are provided for groups rather than for individuals. Into this category fall:

- canteen services;
- sports and recreational facilities;
- facilities for the purchase of goods, in particular those produced or sold by the organisation;
- occupational health facilities.

Canteen facilities

Only the smallest organisations tend not to provide any catering facilities for employees. However, canteen facilities can be the most controversial aspect of employee services. As a result many organisations have canteen committees – a specialist form of joint consultation.

Self-check

Why should management feel that the setting up of a canteen committee will assist in reducing the risk of employee dissatisfaction with canteen facilities?

The assumption here is that the presence of employee representatives should ensure that the 'consumer' is represented in decision-making about the provision of services, and that as a result employees will feel that the correct way to voice dissatisfaction is through their representatives. In this way management hope that any grievances can be dealt with systematically.

The practice of using outside catering contractors has increased. Professionalism, bulk buying and economies of scale in other aspects of catering provision frequently result in such contractors being able to run the canteen cheaper than can the employer. However, employees still will complain to the employer if the service is inadequate.

Activity

Ask someone with responsibility for the provision of catering facilities in your organisation (or in an organisation known to you) to list three reasons why management should make such facilities available to employees.

ANSWER

- Their cost can be offset against corporation tax and therefore they are relatively cheap to provide.
- They help the image of the organisation as a good employer.
- The provision of adequate catering facilities on the premises may reduce the attraction of nearby restaurants and pubs. As a result employees will be less likely to take over-long lunch-breaks!

Sports and social facilities

Welfare services for employees originated at the end of the

nineteenth century, when provision of state services in this general area was sparser than today. Many paternalistic employers opened sports and social clubs for employees and their families. Today not only has provision by local authorities increased, but the recreational and social habits of the population have changed. Many employees like to spend their leisure time away from premises provided by the employer. Some employers have kept their facilities but have made them more open to the public at large.

Facilities for the purchase of goods

Some companies run 'staff shops' where goods produced by the employer or associated employers can be purchased at a discount and provide facilities for personal services, such as banking or hairdressing.

Occupational health facilities

Each year, about 350 million working days are lost because of sickness and industrial injuries. In most years this is over thirty times the working days lost through strikes. It makes economic sense for employers to provide occupational health services for employees. In Europe such services are usually a legal requirement.

Self-check

List three aims of an occupational health service.

ANSWER

- To assist in the establishment and maintenance of the highest possible physical and mental health of employees.
- To ensure that employees' health allows them to cope with their jobs.
- To protect employees from any health hazard which may arise from their jobs.

The interpretation of such aims will differ from one organisation to another. Where the nature of the work is inherently hazardous, more attention is given to the provision of occupational health services.

Many employers see occupational health provision as an educational or preventive service and therefore may include medical screening and counselling on smoking, alcohol and diet. Increasing attention is being given to work-related stress.

Status considerations

In the UK it has been customary to stratify employee services provision and fringe benefits according to the status of employees. This is a reflection of our class structure. Recently many employers have moved towards single status for all employees, though often this excludes senior management, who retain rights to 'top-hat' pension schemes, separate car parks and other symbols of position.

Differences in the provision of employee benefits and facilities have been a source of discontent. Yet moves to 'single staff status' may also be a cause of grievances for higher-grade employees who resent the loss of status differentials. Change in this area needs careful handling by management usually in consultation or negotiation with trade unions.

The future of employee services

Self-check

From the information provided in this chapter, identify two trends likely to affect the provision of employee services in the next five years.

ANSWER

- State welfare provision is unlikely to improve and may decline further. Employers may feel a responsibility to fill gaps in state provision for their employees.
- As organisations become more capital-intensive, i.e. as the amount of financial investment per employee increases, so it becomes relatively cheaper to provide a full range of employee services.

Review

Which of the following statements about the provision of welfare services to employees are true and which are false?

1 All organisations provide a range of welfare services for their employees. *True or false?*
2 When managers undertake career or redundancy counselling they should persuade employees to accept the solution which is in the interests of the employing organisation. *True or false?*
3 Even though they are not professionally trained, employees can counsel each other on career development. *True or false?*
4 Employers often provide pre-retirement courses for employees. *True or false?*
5 Good sports and social facilities encourage loyalty to the organisation by its employees. *True or false?*

ANSWERS

1 False. Probably most organisations do provide such services; small companies will be the exception.
2 False. Counsellors should encourage clients to reach their own solutions. In practice, of course, many managers will be tempted to act in the way suggested in this statement!
3 True.
4 True.
5 Probably false. Whilst such facilities are unlikely to motivate employees to be more productive, they are equally unlikely to demotivate them. Sports and social clubs may be an aid to recruitment and public relations in the locality.

11 | The law and the rights of the individual employee

One of the complexities of employment law is that the length of service required before workers acquire particular legal rights varies quite considerably. The following checklist summarises the current position.

Checklist of individual employment rights

When someone applies for a job, they are protected from:

- race and sex discrimination;
- the 'need' to declare 'spent' offences.

On starting work, employees are entitled to:

- protection against dismissal or other unfavourable treatment on grounds of race, sex or trade union activity;
- equal pay (for both men and women);
- paid time off for antenatal care;
- paid time off for trade union duties*;
- time off for trade union activities*;
- time off for public duties*;
- an itemised pay statement*;
- monetary compensation if the employer fails to give the necessary statutory notice in cases of redundancy;
- monetary compensation if the employer becomes insolvent;
- statutory sick pay provided that they earn more than the 'lower earnings limit'.

With service, employees accrue additional rights, as follows:

After 4 weeks:
- a minimum period of notice;
- guarantee payments and protection from dismissal, if the employer cannot provide work;

- monetary compensation and protection from dismissal, if the employer suspends workers on certain medical grounds.

After 13 weeks:
- written particulars of the contract of employment.

After 26 weeks:
- a written statement of the reasons for dismissal.

After 1 year:
- protection from unfair dismissal (provided that the employer has twenty or more workers).

After 2 years:
- maternity pay;
- maternity leave;
- redundancy compensation;
- paid time off to look for work in cases of redundancy.

Most of the rights listed here apply to full-time workers, part-time workers who work more than 16 hours per week, and part-timers who work more than 8 hours a week and have at least 5 years' continuous service. Those asterisked apply only to those who work 16 hours a week or more.

In this chapter we focus on the major legal rights of employees other than those associated with the termination of the contract of employment.

Anti-discrimination legislation and employee rights

Promotion opportunities

In the same way as they must not discriminate against applicants for employment, employers must give equal opportunities for transfer and promotion.

In 1979 nearly half of the 900 platform staff employed by Bradford Metro, the public bus company service in Bradford, West Yorkshire, were of Asian origin. Many of them had ten to fifteen years' service. There were no Asian inspectors and only one West Indian inspector out of fifty people employed in this capacity. An investigation by the Commission for Racial

Equality (CRE) revealed that the district manager instructed interviewers to be cautious in appointing Asian inspectors. Reasons given for this included fear of opposition from white busmen and of problems with the travelling public. As a result higher standards of performance, including those required in a written test, were demanded of Asian applicants.

Self-check

Remembering the discussion of the law on discrimination in Chapter 5, comment on the legality of Bradford Metro's promotion procedures. What action should have been taken to remedy the situation?

The instructions to interviewers are directly discriminatory; the written test is indirectly discriminatory. The CRE, in its investigation, found that Asian applicants did disproportionately badly; the test did not measure relevant abilities and the standard of English demanded was not necessary for effective job performance. The company should devise a more appropriate test.

Other actions taken by Bradford Metro since the CRE investigation include:

- the introduction of an equal opportunities policy;
- a programme of language training for Asian busmen to improve their chances of promotion;
- training for managers and supervisors in managing a multi-racial workforce.

A higher proportion of Asians and West Indians are now inspectors.

Training

Legislation protects employees who believe themselves to have been denied equal opportunities for training. In addition the Sex Discrimination Act and the Race Relations Act include positive discrimination provisions, where during the previous year there were no (or comparatively few) persons of one sex or race doing a particular type of work. In such circumstances the provision of special training programmes is permissible. This is the only legal provision for positive discrimination in the UK at present. Once members of minority groups have received training, they must be selected for jobs on merit alone.

Benefits, facilities and services

Employees must give equal access to fringe benefits to all their employees. Thus it would be illegal for a bank to offer low-cost mortgages to male employees only.

Genuine occupational qualifications

Review

A newspaper publisher wishes to promote a journalist to the position of Middle East correspondent. Would it be illegal to consider only men for the job?

No, since the job will involve work in countries whose laws or customs make it impossible for a woman to do the job effectively.

The equality commissions

The Equal Opportunities Commission (EOC) and the Commission for Racial Equality (CRE) are charged with the identification and elimination of obstacles to equality of opportunity. Their members and employees operate independently of the government, though they are paid by the state. They must keep relevant legislation under review and where necessary suggest amendments. There is also a responsibility to promote research and educational activities. The commissions can draw up codes of practice giving practical guidance on the elimination of discrimination. Such codes are not legally binding, but are admissible in evidence before an industrial tribunal or court.

Both commissions can conduct formal investigations, either on their own initiative or at the request of the Secretary of State for Employment. There have been a number of such investigations into employment practices. Where evidence of unlawful discrimination is found, non-discrimination notices can be issued to prevent further discrimination.

Equal pay

Like the Sex Discrimination Act, the Equal Pay Act deals with discrimination at work.

Broadly, the Equal Pay Act deals with wages and other terms and conditions of employment; as we have seen, the Sex Discrimination Act covers the terms of an offer of employment and is concerned with the elimination of discrimination in recruitment, training, promotion and other aspects of the employment relationship.

The Equal Pay Act gives men and women the right to equal treatment in individual contracts of employment. It also provides for references to be made to the Central Arbitration Committee. This is not a court but can amend discriminatory collective agreements or employers' pay structures. In order for such changes to be made by the committee, there must be clauses in the agreement or pay structure which refer only to men or to women.

Self-check

Does the Equal Pay Act apply to all employees?

The Act applies to every male and female employee regardless of length of service or hours worked per week. (If you could not answer this, refer to the checklist of employee rights at the beginning of this chapter.) Here we shall discuss the law as if we were dealing with a woman's claim for equal pay.

Claims under the Equal Pay Act

It is up to the applicant for equal pay to select the male worker with whom she wishes to compare herself in order to make a claim. He must be employed by the same or an associated employer and normally he must work at the same place as her; she and he must be employed under the same terms and conditions of employment. It is possible to make a comparison with a male predecessor but only if he occupied the job in the recent past.

Having found a man with whom to compare herself, the employee must be able to show that she is employed:

- on 'like work' to that of a man; *or*
- in a job which, though different from that of a man, has been rated as equivalent under a job evaluation scheme; *or*
- under the Equal Pay Act (Amendment) Regulations, on work of equal value to a man's in terms of the demands on her under such headings as effort, skill and decision-making; in such cases there need not be a job evaluation scheme, or where there is, she can claim that it has discriminatory results.

'Like work' 'Like work' is defined by the Act as being of 'the same or broadly similar nature' to the man's work. The courts have said that tribunals need not undertake a minute examination of the differences between the work done by the woman and that done by the man. For example, a cook who prepared meals for an executive dining-room compared her work with that of an assistant chef in the works canteen. Differences in the hours worked and in the volume and nature of the meals prepared, were felt to be insufficient justification for unequal pay. That is, they were not of 'practical importance'.

The points which tribunals consider to determine whether differences are of practical importance are:

- the nature of the differences;
- whether they occur in practice;
- how often they occur;
- whether the differences are sufficiently significant to justify differences in terms and conditions of employment.

Some tribunals have used as a yardstick whether two men would be paid differently if they did the jobs in question.

Work 'rated as equivalent' This is a very limited point of access to equal pay for most women. First, the organisation concerned must have a job evaluation scheme and both the woman's job and that of the man with whom she chooses to compare herself must be covered by it. Surveys suggest that, while the majority of large employers use such techniques, many small ones do not. Secondly, an examination of legal judgements reveals that, once job evaluation schemes have been designed and implemented, it is very difficult to challenge them, unless it can be shown that there has been a failure to apply the scheme in accordance with its rules.

'Equal pay for work of equal value' Because the UK is a member of the European Economic Community, its legislation can be challenged in the European Court of Justice. In 1982 this court ruled that because the Equal Pay Act does not entitle a woman to claim equal pay for work of equal value unless her employer uses a job evaluation scheme, UK legislation failed to comply with EEC law. As a result the Equal Pay Act has been amended. A woman who cannot achieve equal pay by either of the routes described above may achieve it if a tribunal considers that her job is of 'equal value' to that of the man with whom she compares herself. This route can be used where there is no job evaluation scheme or where the woman wishes to challenge an existing job evaluation scheme as discriminatory. Comparisons may be made between jobs covered by different evaluation schemes or pay structures. Independent experts approved by ACAS are used by tribunals to determine whether the two jobs are of equal value.

Genuine material differences Even where the tribunal agrees that two jobs are 'broadly similar', 'rated as equivalent under a job evaluation scheme' or of 'equal value', the employer can avoid equal pay by proving that there is a 'genuine material difference' between them. For example, if the woman has less experience than the man or is younger than him and these are relevant factors in determining pay, then it would be reasonable in law to pay less to the woman than to the man. For equal value claims the employee must show that the difference in pay is due to sex discrimination.

Maternity rights legislation

Self-check

List three legal rights of female employees during pregnancy and early motherhood.

ANSWER

- Maternity leave.
- Maternity pay.
- Paid time off for antenatal care.

You may have also listed the right not to be unfairly dismissed because of pregnancy. This is covered in Chapter 15.

Maternity leave

A woman who has two years' continuous service by the eleventh week before her baby is due has the right to return to work after the birth, provided that she:

- gives 21 days' notice in writing of resignation due to pregnancy, states the intention to return and gives the date when the baby is expected;
- confirms within 14 days that she still intends to return to work in reply to a letter from her employer 49 days after the date when the baby was due;
- gives her employer at least 21 days' notice of her intention to return to work.

Normally women return to work 29 weeks after the date of the baby's birth. They are not prevented in law from 'keeping their options open' by telling employers that they intend to return to work and then changing their mind once the baby is born.

The employer must allow the woman to return to her previous job unless it is not 'reasonably practicable'. In such cases she must be offered suitable alternative work, i.e. the terms and conditions of employment must not be substantially less favourable than they would have been had she gone back to her previous job.

> ### Self-check
>
> Before pregnancy, Jane worked as secretary to the personnel manager of British Industrial Chemicals. On her return from maternity leave she is offered a job as secretary to the computer manager. She does not like the latter and refuses to accept the job. What is her position in law?

She would be regarded as having acted unreasonably, if the job was broadly the same and carried the same pay and other terms and conditions of employment. An argument that she did not like the manager would not be reasonable. However, if the job was not at the same location or required her to work substantially different hours her refusal would probably be judged reasonable.

Maternity pay

The service qualification for maternity pay is the same as for maternity leave and is only available to women who have given 21 days' notice of the date on which they expect to stop work. Maternity pay is normally nine-tenths of the weekly wage. The employer must make the payment but can reclaim it in full from the state maternity fund.

Paid time off for antenatal care

Reasonable time off is available to pregnant women for antenatal care. The employer may ask for proof both of pregnancy and of the date and time of appointments.

Other rights to time off from work

> ### Self-check
>
> List three reasons which entitle employees to time off from work, other than for antenatal care.

ANSWER

● Paid time off for trade union duties.

- Time off for trade union activities.
- Time off for public duties.

You may also have included paid time off to look for another job in cases of redundancy. This is covered in Chapter 15.

Time off for trade union duties

Trade union representatives have the right to paid time off for duties connected with industrial relations in the organisation in which they work. This includes:

- collective bargaining with management;
- communicating with members about such negotiations;
- consulting full-time officers;
- dealing with members' grievances and disciplinary cases;
- attending relevant training courses.

Safety representatives also have rights to paid time off to perform their functions.

Time off for trade union activities

Members of trade unions recognised by the employer for collective bargaining purposes have the right to unpaid time off to take part in the activities of the union. These activities include:

- attending a conference as a union delegate;
- attending union meetings;
- voting in union elections.

There is no right to time off for anything connected with industrial action.

Some clarification of these legal provisions can be found in the ACAS code of practice, *Time Off for Trade Union Duties and Activities*.

Time off for public duties

Employees are entitled to reasonable time off without pay to perform the following duties:

- justice of the peace;
- member of a local authority;
- member of any statutory tribunal;
- member of a health authority;
- member of the governing body of an educational establish-ment maintained by a local educational authority;
- member of a water authority;
- jury service;
- member of the voluntary reserve forces.

Sick pay and medical suspension

Employers are responsible for the payment of statutory sick pay (SSP) for the first eight weeks of sickness. The full amount of such payments can be recouped from the state. Such payments are related to earnings. However, many employees have con-tractual rights to sick pay over and above those laid down in this legislation. The regulations governing SSP are complex. If you are concerned with this area of employment you should ensure that you are fully conversant with the details.

Suspension from work on medical grounds

Workers whose health has been put at risk by exposure to hazardous materials must be taken off their normal jobs and may be suspended from work on full pay for up to six months. Management can offer suitable alternative work which may or may not be within the terms of the employees' contracts. (The legal definition of 'suitable alternative work' is discussed on p. 260 in relation to redundancy.)

There are detailed regulations covering this area of employ-ment law. However, it should be recognised that the number of workers covered by them is very small. You should check whether employees for whom you have responsibility are covered.

Self-check

You are a manager in a nuclear power station. Workers for whom you have responsibility wear film badges which indicate their level of exposure to radiation. The badges show that the limit has been exceeded. What should you do?

You should ensure that they are suspended on full pay, or offer them suitable alternative work, until a doctor authorises their return.

Payments to workers when there is no work to do

Management has no right to suspend employees, cut their minimum rate of pay, introduce short-time working or lay them off unless this is provided for in their contracts of employment. However, many agreements with trade unions do provide for guaranteed minimum earnings during a period of lay-off. In addition workers are entitled in law to minimum 'guarantee payments' for days when no work is provided. These statutory payments are very small. Frequently collective agreements provide for higher payments in these circumstances.

The limits of employment law

You may have gained the impression that the employment relationship is greatly influenced by legislation. Certainly since 1963, when employees got rights to minimum periods of notice, there has been a vast increase in the importance of this area of labour law. However, much of the relationship between management and employees is untouched by legislation.

Did you know?

The UK and Denmark are the only EEC countries which have no general legislation on hours of work. In this country only women, young people and some occupational groups such as drivers are protected in this way. Nor is there legislation fixing the length of holidays. Again, most European countries have a legal minimum number of days of holiday.

There is no national minimum wage in the UK, though about three million workers do have their wages fixed by wages councils. These bodies do give some protection, but not all vulnerable workers are covered and in many cases the statutory minimum rates laid down by the wages councils are deplorably low. There has been opposition to a national minimum wage and other minimum terms and conditions of employment because of the fear that additional unemployment that could result. This is a debatable point which we do not have space for here.

Review

Do you remember Fred's Food Processing Company in Chapter 8? There we learned that Fred was opening a chain of frozen food shops. That was two years' ago. Now he has six shops in a number of towns in the Midlands. He has recruited staff for the shops and for the distribution side of the business.

You are asked to examine the legal implications of some of his current problems with employees.

1 A female check-out operator in one of the shops, who has six months' service, claims equal pay with a male storekeeper in the manufacturing company. There is no job evaluation scheme and Fred has separate bargaining arrangements with the unions for his retail business and his manufacturing company.

2 Fred's secretary is expecting a baby. She has three years' service with the company and says that she wishes to take maternity leave. She is not married. Fred says that she cannot return to work as his secretary since he disapproves of her behaviour, and anyway it is unreasonable to expect him to hold the job open. He cannot manage with a temporary replacement.

3 One of the shop stewards in the manufacturing company notifies Fred that he will be attending an advanced shop steward training course. Fred says that the steward knows quite enough already and that he never gets a full day's work out of him!

4 One of the frozen food shop supervisors tells him that she has been elected as a parent governor at her daughter's school. She will need one day off work a term to fulfil this

responsibility. He says that this is monstrous! How is he supposed to cope without the regular attendance of key employees? On reflection he agrees that she can have the time off without pay.

ANSWERS

1 Clearly this claim is not covered by the definition of 'like work' or 'work rated as equivalent' following a job evaluation study. Whether it is 'work of equal value' would depend on the view of an independent expert. Even then she might not get equal pay if Fred could show that there was a 'genuine material difference' between her work and that of the storekeeper.

2 Fred's secretary's pregnancy. Her unmarried status is ir- relevant. Since she has the necessary two years' service she is entitled to maternity leave. Fred can refuse to have her back as his secretary if it is not 'reasonably practicable' for him to do so. In that case he must offer her 'suitable alternative work'. That is, the work which she is offered must be 'not less favour- able' than if she had not been absent.

3 Whether or not the training course is a trade union duty would depend on whether the course is recognised by the union to which the steward belongs and whether it is relevant to his duties as a shop steward. Fred can ask to see the syllabus.

4 In law this would be classified as a public duty. Hence she is entitled to reasonable time off without pay in order to fulfil the demands of the role. It is likely that the small amount of time she is said to need here would be considered reasonable.

12 | Fair pay and employee benefits at work

The assumption behind most reward systems is that pay is a key motivator.

> *Review*
>
> Would you agree that pay is a key motivator?

In chapter 6 we concluded that, whilst there are motivators other than money, pay is a major factor in the employment relationship. It is management's task to find the package of inducements which prompts maximum employee productivity.

By the end of this chapter you should be able to :

- discuss the factors which affect the level of wages and salaries;
- define 'job evaluation' and discuss some of the major methods;
- appreciate the range of payment systems which management uses to encourage employee productivity;
- list some of the most common fringe benefits and discuss their effectiveness in encouraging employee commitment.

To be effective, reward systems must fit particular organisational circumstances and be reviewed regularly.

Factors affecting salary and wage levels

> *Activity*
>
> Ask a personnel specialist or trade union representative to tell you about the factors which affect the level of wages or salaries in your organisation (or in one with which you are familiar). After your discussion list four such factors.

Those you listed should be included here:

- the importance of the job or the individual to the organisation;
- the strength of trade unions representing workers;
- the productivity of the individual or group;
- any minimum rate of pay laid down by law;
- the profitability of the organisation;
- national pay norms which often are an integral part of government economic policy.

Summarising, pay levels reflect the rate for labour in the external 'market', internal organisational factors mainly associated with the establishment and maintenance of pay differentials, and individual factors associated with performance and commitment as demonstrated, for example, by length of service. The level of pay can be seen as the result of interaction between management's desire to obtain maximum employee productivity at minimum cost and employees' wishes for the highest possible reward for the least effort.

In crudest terms the contract of employment can be seen as a wage–effort bargain – see figure 21. In other words, wages are exchanged for effort.

The wage–effort bargain

When an individual joins an organisation as a paid employee, he enters a contract of employment. The employer expects him to exert himself in pursuit of the objectives of the organisation; the employee expects to be fairly rewarded. The rewards may be:

- money;
- status;
- a sense of achievement, etc.

The complexity of the relationship lies in the fact that not all employees expect similar rewards. Also, management is usually not too specific about the effort required from the employee.

> *Self-check*
>
> Why is this?

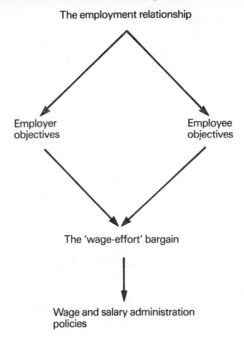

Figure 21. The wage–effort bargain

Management wishes to use labour flexibly so that new requirements can be placed on employees as working processes or organisational structures change.

> ### Activity
>
> Look at the job description for your current job. (If you are not working at present, look at that of a friend.) How does your employer ensure that you can be used in a flexible manner whilst laying on you specific job responsibilities?

The answer usually lies in an 'any other duties as required by management' clause in a job description.

Wage and salary administration policies

Self-check

Taking into account our brief discussion of the factors which influence pay levels and the nature of the wage–effort bargain, list three possible objectives for management in devising remuneration policies.

The list of possible objectives is long, reflecting the complexity of this area of personnel management:

- to attract sufficient suitable employees;
- to encourage effective employees to remain in the organisation's employment;
- to obtain optimal performance from employees;
- to encourage employees to improve their performance;
- to have sufficient flexibility to reward high performers and deal with poor performers;
- to operate within the framework of current employment legislation and national economic policy where relevant;
- to operate at minimum cost;
- to ensure that jobs of equivalent value to the organisation are rewarded equally;
- to ensure that employees feel fairly rewarded for the jobs they do.

These are broad policy objectives likely to be supported by most managers. Their conversion into practice will depend on the relative priorities accorded to them in light of organisational circumstances. For example, a company struggling for survival will place greater emphasis on operating at minimum cost and paying the lowest possible wages, rather than on the attraction and retention of employees who feel fairly rewarded for their efforts.

According to its policy objectives, management is likely to be concerned with three issues in the establishment of fair pay:

- wage or salary relativities – to ensure that what is paid is fair by comparison with payments received by other employees within the organisation;

- to ensure that pay is fair in comparison with other employers;
- methods of payment which encourage effective performance and commitment by individuals or work groups.

This can be expressed diagramatically – see figure 22.

Figure 22. Wage and salary administration policies and practices

Job evaluation and the design of pay structures

Bernard Shaw in *Everybody's Political What's What* challenged the possibility of being able to 'assess in pounds, shillings and pence the difference between the social service of an archbishop and a turf bookmaker or to fix a just wage for poets laureate and sausage makers'. Job evaluation attempts to establish the relative value of jobs to the employing organisation in which they are situated. In the UK there has been no attempt to undertake a national exercise of the type required to meet Shaw's challenge.

What is job evaluation?

- *Job evaluation is not an exact science – it relies on subjective judgement.*

In measuring the relative value of jobs, job evaluation requires the subjective, though systematic, exercise of judgement in identifying and assessing differences between jobs. It only works effectively if those involved believe it to be fair.

- *Job evaluation is not a method of determining rates of pay.*

Job evaluation precedes pay determination. After the relative value of jobs to the organisation has been established, they are usually grouped into grades or categories. Pay is attached to these. Where trade unions are recognised for collective bargaining purposes, this is done by negotiation.

- *Job evaluation is not concerned with the performance of the individual employee.*

Rather it is concerned with the demands of the job. Whether the individual carries out the job adequately should be immaterial. Good performance may be rewarded by merit payments but job evaluation is concerned with the value of the job relative to other jobs and not with the relative value of the employee as compared with other employees.

Self-check

Is it easy to make the distinction between the requirements of the job and the performance of the job holder?

It is not, particularly in the case of managerial or professional jobs, where the individual to some degree defines the nature of the tasks performed. Nevertheless, for job evaluation purposes, it is important to attempt the distinction.

In sum, job evaluation attempts to answer three questions critical to the management of people:

- What is the relative value of a job to the organisation?
- How can this value be determined?

- How can this be done in a way which is accepted as fair by most employees?

Job evaluation can be effective as a means of answering these questions only if it is part of what might be termed a 'total system of remuneration and motivation'.

> ## Self-check
>
> List four other personnel management techniques which we have discussed so far in this book and which also should be part of this system.

- work restructuring techniques;
- performance appraisal;
- career development;
- employee services.

The process of job evaluation

No matter which of the many available methods is used the process of job evaluation must contain certain basic steps. Figure 23 emphasises the importance of obtaining much information about jobs before attempting to evaluate their relative value. We have already discussed job analysis and the writing of job descriptions. To encourage employees to believe in the fairness of the results of job evaluation, care must be taken at this stage to involve them or their representatives. Also, this task should not be given to untrained employees or to line managers.

> ## Self-check
>
> List three ways in which jobs can be analysed for job evaluation purposes so as to encourage employee involvement.

ANSWER

- Employees can be asked to complete questionnaires on the demands of their jobs. These can be accompanied by a job

Job analysis

Job description

Select benchmark
jobs

Job evaluation

Job grading

Pay determination

Figure 23. The process of job evaluation

description and signed by both the job holder and the line manager to indicate that the information presented is accurate.

- Job holders can be interviewed by a job analyst who then compiles the information on the demands of the job for signature as above.
- Job holders can be observed at work by job analysts who again compile information for job evaluation purposes. This method may be suitable only for manual jobs where activities are directly observable.

Job evaluation is most often used in medium or large organisations. In such cases it is most convenient to select a sample (ten to thirty) of 'benchmark' jobs at this stage as a basis for the establishment of the job evaluation system. Benchmark jobs should be:

- well known to the evaluators;
- representative of the level and type of jobs to be evaluated;
- not the subject of a current dispute between management and employees.

Now job evaluation, using one of the methods discussed below, can take place.

This will result in the establishment of a rank order of jobs in the organisation from the lowest to the highest job evaluated. After this the jobs in the hierarchy are grouped into grades. Only then is the pay for grades established either by negotiation or by managerial judgement.

Methods of job evaluation

There are two main ways of evaluating jobs – analytical and non-analytical. Analytical methods break jobs down into their constituent parts for assessment purposes; non-analytical methods evaluate jobs as wholes.

Non-analytical methods

Job ranking This is the simplest method of job evaluation. Each job is assessed as a whole in relation to the others. Jobs thus evaluated are listed in terms of their importance. There is no analysis other than the opinion and decision of the evaluators.

Self-check

Suppose we use job ranking to assess four jobs. The rank order we establish is:

Electrician.
Cook.
Kitchen assistant.
Cleaner.

What will be a problem of putting this result into practice?

The most obvious problem is that there is no indication as to how much more important one job is than the next in the hierarchy. So this can be a very blunt and biased evaluation tool. Its results may be questioned. It may be appropriate to the needs of the very small company, however.

Paired comparisons This is a form of job ranking but with an element of scoring which measures whether a job is more important than, less important than or as important as another job, so producing a final league table of jobs. Again this non-analytical method tends to be used in small companies, though it can be applied in larger ones using benchmark jobs.

Self-check

List three advantages of the paired comparison method of job evaluation.

ANSWER

It is quick and cheap to use, and easy to understand.

On the other hand, it is crude and insufficiently analytic to be likely to be very convincing to employees.

Job classification This is not a form of job evaluation as such but really a categorisation of jobs within broadly defined grades. It is used in the Civil Service and in teaching. Once the number of grades to be used has been determined a general job description for each grade is prepared. Here is an example from a well-known classification system:

Level 3
Tasks calling for independent arrangement of work and exercise of some initiative, where supervision is needed. Detailed familiarity with one or more branches of established procedure required.

Self-check

Can you see a problem in applying this definition to jobs?

It could be argued that it is rather broad and that quite different responsibilities could be grouped within it. Yet in certain circumstances it may be too rigid, leading to the exclusion of jobs on seemingly trivial grounds. Recently some companies have moved towards more analytical methods because these problems have made it difficult to encompass rapid changes in technology and the attendant more complex job descriptions. On the other hand, job classification systems are simple and cheap to administer.

Analytical methods

Here jobs are assessed and numerical values given under a number of separate headings such as decision-making, working conditions and knowledge required. In this way, by comparing total numerical values, assessors can gauge how much more difficult and responsible one job is than another; very different jobs can be compared.

Points rating

Points rating enables evaluators to give a points score to each job. There is no standardised points system available for all organisations and many use more than one system.

Stages of designing and implementing a points rating scheme

1 Establish a representative committee It is very common for schemes to be designed and implemented by joint management–union working groups as part of the process of attempting to ensure that the results of job evaluation are perceived as fair.

2 Analyse a significant sample of jobs and write job descriptions Benchmark jobs should be selected according to the criteria listed on p. 195.

3 Select and define those criteria considered most critical in determining differences between jobs This is difficult. Too many factors will make the scheme over-complex and may lead to elements of certain jobs being counted twice, so that the objectivity of the scheme may be cast in doubt. Too few factors may make it difficult to cover the full range of jobs effectively. It may be helpful to look at schemes used in the same industry or for similar occupation groups when designing a scheme. Great care must be taken to define each factor so that it can be applied to each job covered by the scheme.

4 Weight factors and convert to points Commonly certain factors have a higher number of points allocated than others, reflecting the relative importance an organisation attaches to a particular factor. Here is a list of factors which the joint management–union working group in Colin's Cars, a manufacturer of sports cars, has decided should be used to evaluate all the non-manual jobs in the company:

- education;
- experience;
- specialised knowledge;
- complexity of task;
- communication – contacts and relationships;
- management of people;
- supervision received;
- physical environment.

The next task of the group is to attach weights to the factors.

> *Self-check*
>
> Imagine that you are a member of the working group at Colin's Cars. Rank these factors in order of importance. Then using 100 points allocate the number of points to each factor which you think it is worth. You must use all the points.

In many ways this is a trick exercise since, without an intimate knowledge of Colin's Cars, you are unable to weight the factors. However, this would be a useful exercise for members of the working group to undertake to come up with some trial weightings. There is no correct answer. All that can be said is that the right weightings are those which ultimately produce an acceptable ranking of jobs.

After weights have been allocated, each factor definition will have to be subdivided into degrees, and these, like the factors, will have to be defined. Here are the factor and subfactor definitions for 'specialised knowledge' in the points rating scheme being designed for use in Colin's Cars:

Specialised knowledge (weighting 8 per cent)

This factor appraises the requirement for specialised knowledge or techniques which it is essential for a job holder to have.

Level:
1 No specialised knowledge required.
2 Some specialised knowledge or understanding of techniques and terminology to a working standard.
3 A higher level of specialised knowledge or understanding of techniques and terminology to a working standard.
4 A good 'in-depth' level of specialised knowledge or understanding of techniques and terminology such that some guidance and interpretation may be given to others.
5 Specialist knowledge and techniques associated with the job are required to be very well understood in great depth and detail so that available information can not only be well understood and interpreted but also translated into instructions for the guidance of others.

In points rating schemes it is quite common for a total of 500 points to be used. Thus a maximum of 40 points would be allocated to 'specialised knowledge' in this example.

> *Self-check*
>
> Suppose the working group decides to allocate points evenly across the levels of this factor. How many points would be given to a job which was felt to fit level 3 in terms of the specialised knowledge required of the job holder?

The answer is 20, since no points would be allocated to level 1, 10 to level 2 and so on up to the maximum of 40 at level 5.

5 Test-run a selection of jobs The benchmark jobs are evaluated using the newly designed scheme.

6 Compare with the established hierarchy of jobs It cannot be stressed too often that job evaluation schemes only work effectively if the results are acceptable to employees. It is necessary to assess the likelihood of the system producing acceptable results. To do this the points allocated to each job in the test run are plotted against rates presently paid to job holders – see figure 24.

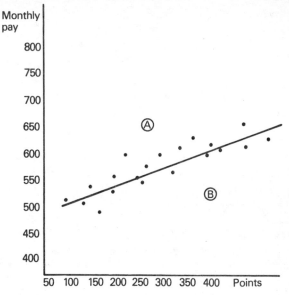

Figure 24. Scattergram of the relationship between points and existing pay levels

A line of 'best fit' can be drawn through the points indicating those jobs which are out of line. In this table jobs *A* and *B* are out of line and are known as 'red circle' and 'green circle' jobs respectively.

> ## Self-check
>
> What does the job evaluation scheme show about the pay currently associated with jobs *A* and *B*?

Job *A* is overpaid and job *B* is underpaid, since in theory the introduction of the job evaluation scheme should be self-financing in that the cost of bringing green circle jobs up to the line of best fit should be balanced by the savings derived from reducing the pay associated with red circle jobs.

Self-check

Will this happen in practice?

Usually there is a 'buying-in' cost; the wages bill will increase at the time that the new scheme is introduced. Normally the pay of holders of red circle jobs is frozen until cost-of-living increases catch up with them. Holders of green circle jobs may be given pay increases.

7 Adjust factor weights and points There may not be such a good fit between points and pay as that indicated in figure 24. In this case stages **5, 6** and **7** may have to be repeated until an acceptable result is obtained.

8 Evaluate all jobs The remaining jobs should fall close to the line of best fit which has already been established. Red circle and green circle jobs will have to be dealt with as indicated above.

9 Divide the jobs into grades The points scores provide a basis for determining the grades which will encompass groups of similar jobs. Careful thought must be given to both the break points between the grades and the numbers of grades.

Activity

If your organisation, or one known to you, has a points rating system, talk to a personnel specialist, a line manager or a trade union representative about how it works. Then list two advantages and two disadvantages of this method of job evaluation.

ADVANTAGES

- It encourages careful analysis of job content.
- A rationale is provided as to why one job is graded higher than another.
- It seems to be more objective than non-analytical methods.
- It can be used to measure the value of new jobs and thus can accommodate technological change.

- It can cover a wide range of jobs.
- A points rating scheme can be devised to meet the characteristics of jobs in a particular organisation.

DISADVANTAGES

- It can give a spurious impression of mathematical accuracy. Like all job evaluation methods, it is subjective.
- It is time-consuming and therefore expensive, particularly if a large number of factors are used.
- In practice it is difficult to make a points rating system cover a very wide range of jobs – from managerial to manual, for example – because of the difficulty of weighting factors where one set of factors may be more relevant to one category of jobs than to another.
- To be seen to be fair, management (and trade unions where relevant) may wish to give employees information about the system. This is likely to lead to problems, for example in justifying factor weightings.

In conclusion it should be said that points rating is probably the most popular method of job evaluation.

Checklist of questions for management and personnel specialists contemplating the introduction of job evaluation

- Which method should we use?
- Should we use management consultants and if so in what capacity?
- Which categories of employees do we want the scheme to cover?
- Will more than one scheme be needed to cover all employees?
- Shall we involve trade unions or other employee representatives? If so, to what extent?
- What shall be the constitution of any working group needed to design and implement the scheme?
- Who can be used as job analysts and what training will they need?
- Who will be the job evaluators and what training will they need?

- What training will managers and union representatives, other than those directly involved, need?
- Who will do all this training?
- How much information about job evaluation should we communicate to employees?
- What mechanism should we use to review the scheme to ensure that once it is implemented it works effectively?

More questions could be added to this list. From this section you will have understood that job evaluation can be complex and that great care must be taken in the design and implementation of schemes.

External pay comparisons

After the relative value of jobs to the organisation has been determined, we must find out what effect market rates are likely to have on the pay structure as a whole.

Self-check

Is there a market rate for a job?

No, there is always a range of rates paid by different employers, either because the duties performed, even where the job title is the same, vary somewhat or because wage and salary policies of employers differ, as suggested on pp. 191–2.

Market rate surveys

It will be necessary to use market rate surveys to develop and maintain competitive salary and wage structures.

Activity

Talk to someone in your personnel department to find out which sources they use to obtain data on market rates. Then list three sources of such information.

I thought of four sources:

- Company surveys. Sometimes companies form a 'club' for the exchange of this sort of information.
- General published surveys. These usually give information by industrial sector, size of organisation and job title. Sometimes information on employee benefits is also included.
- Specialised surveys. These are carried out by professional bodies, trade unions and employers' or trade associations.
- Analysis of job advertisements. This information is more problematic than the other sources since job descriptions may be 'glossy' to attract candidates, and salary data is often incomplete or inflated.

You should be aware of the inexact nature of this information. The skill is to extract a market rate for a job which is a reasonable compromise between all available data. In making such judgements the following questions will be helpful:

- Does the survey show a single rate or a range for a particular job?
- When was it carried out? Has it been updated since?
- Is the sample sufficiently large to be representative of the organisations, jobs, locations and so on which you require?
- Is the pay data comparable, i.e. are overtime, shift pay and other additions to normal earnings clearly indicated?
- Is information available on employee benefits?
- Are job descriptions available and not just job titles?
- For what purpose is the information produced – as a service or to exchange information? Are there other purposes, for example consultants attempting to attract clients?
- Is the information clear and easy to understand?
- Is the survey value for money?

Salary and wage administration

Internal pay relativities can be established by job evaluation and then related to the external market for labour by the use of wage and salary surveys. Final pay levels will then be established either by managerial judgement or by negotiation with recognised trade unions. So far as manual jobs are concerned, this may be the end of the story, since there is likely to be a rate for the job regardless of length of service or performance. For non-manual workers it is more likely that, for each grade of job, there will be an associated salary range with a minimum and a maximum rate of pay. It is assumed that all jobs within the grade or band are of roughly equivalent value to the organisation, but that the salary of individuals in the same job grade may vary.

 Self-check

 List two reasons for such variations in the pay of individuals whose jobs fall within the same grade.

Progression through grades may be entirely on the basis of managerial judgement of 'merit' or automatically with length of service. Trade unions have tended to prefer the latter method since it restricts the prerogative of management to show favouritism. Very often there is an overlap between the salary range associated with one grade and that of adjacent grades.

 Self-check

 Why should this be?

The rationale is that an employee with much experience in a job at one level is worth more to the organisation than a new recruit to a job in the grade above.

A further design feature of salary structures to which management should give attention is the width of the grade bands. Broad bands emphasise the performance of the individual within the grade whereas narrow bands place more importance on the level of the job and on promotion from one category to another. In many organisations narrow grade bands are more common for junior staff, recognising that there are limited variations in performance at this level. For more senior staff broad bands are felt to be needed for the recognition of individual responsibility. Sometimes there is provision to pay exceptional staff more than the top of the salary scale of the grade in which their job falls.

Pay incentives

Job evaluation is used frequently to give a structure for basic pay.

However, other pay elements are often added to this. One of the most common, for production employees in particular, has tended to be incentive payments directly related to the effort expended by the individual or the work group.

Piecework

Sometimes the term 'piecework' is used to describe incentive payment systems.

> *Self-check*
>
> Attempt a definition of 'piecework'.

'Piecework' is literally work for which payment is by the piece of work produced.

> *Self-check*
>
> Can you think of any workers who even today are paid on a pure piecework basis?

The only category that comes to mind are homeworkers, mainly women, who work in their own homes often on very routine tasks such as envelope addressing or garment making. Rates of pay for this work are lamentably low. Employees paid only on the basis of output have no basic earnings by which to support their everyday living requirements.

Payment by results

Here the incentive element normally comprises no more than 25 per cent of the pay packet and this proportion is tending to decline as a proportion of total earnings.

> *Self-check*
>
> Why do you think this is?

As much manual work has become subject to technological change, it has become more machine-paced. As a result the individual employee has a decreasing ability to affect the amount of production. In these circumstances payment by results becomes less appropriate.

The mechanics of payment by results systems

Work study or management services specialists play a prominent role in the operation of most payment by results systems. These rest on the concept of a 'standard time' – the time necessary for an appropriately qualified operator to complete a clearly defined task at an acceptable level of quality. Time standards are established through the systematic application of work measurement techniques. It is not necessary for the personnel specialist or line manager to understand them in detail since frequently specialists in this area will be available for help.

Effective use of payment by results

Payment by results systems are used primarily in production situations where:

- work cycles are generally short and repetitive;
- output can be measured in terms of units produced;
- work has a high labour content and is not predominantly machine-paced;
- high-quality production is not essential;
- jobs are relatively stable;
- sufficient back-up stocks are available to meet fluctuations in both demand and output.

   Self-check

   Why is this last feature important?

Payment by results systems give employees considerable control over output. If they wish to limit production, either for individual or group reasons, they can do so. Also employees are likely to become very discontented if their bonus earnings are reduced by shortages of components.

Self-check

Mike's Manufacturing produces batches of components for the car industry. The components produced tend to change every six months or so. Is this production system suitable for payment by results?

For management there is the danger that the rates paid for effort expended will be subject to constant renegotiation, especially if unions are well organised. This could lead to inflationary 'wage drift' where wages move upwards regardless of productivity.

Other conditions for the successful introduction of payment by results systems are that:

- cooperation is forthcoming from employees who are not able to participate in the bonus scheme;
- high bonus earnings of individuals or groups will not stimulate pressure for parity from other employees;
- sufficient well-trained work study or management services specialists are employed.

Assumptions behind payment by results

Work-study-based payment by results systems, like job evaluation, are systematic rather than scientific techniques. They are based on the assessment of work study specialists and others of production times and work as incentives only if all concerned believe them to be fair. They are designed on the assumption that the 'carrot' of more pay will encourage workers to greater output.

Self-check

From what you have learned so far in this book about motivation theory, do you think that this assumption is sound?

Our discussions have suggested that the motivation to work is very complex and that, whilst money is an important source of motivation, it is not the only one for all workers at all times.

Research on the effect of incentives suggests the following problems may occur.

Bargaining over rates Work study and management services techniques are subjective though systematic. As a result some jobs are 'tightly' timed whilst others have 'loose' times. It is much more beneficial for the employee to have work for which the times are 'loose'.

Self-check

Why is this?

In these situations it is possible to make more money for less effort. As a result there is likely to be bargaining both over work allocation and over the times allotted to particular jobs.

Work group pressure to keep production down Employees whose output is much higher than the norm of the group are often subject to pressure to reduce their productivity.

Self-check

Why should this be?

Very high output by an individual can endanger bonus earnings in that management may come to believe that all are capable of more effort and may cut the rate paid accordingly.

Employees' dislike of fluctuating earnings Employees attempt to create stabilising devices which may distort management's assessment of output.

Payment by results systems, then, can have disadvantageous effects on workplace industrial relations.

Measured daywork systems

Often these are introduced to overcome the disadvantages of both payment by results and payment on the basis of time. Here pay is fixed at a higher level than management would normally pay to a time-rate worker, on the understanding that performance is maintained at a specific level. Bonus is paid for achieving this level of performance but pay does not fluctuate in the short term with actual performance. If an employee fails consistently to achieve the required standard even after further help and training, a wide range of sanctions are applied – withdrawal or reduction of bonus and ultimately dismissal.

Self-check

In payment by results systems, bonus is the reward for actual performance. For what is bonus paid in measured daywork systems?

It is paid for achieving and maintaining a standard performance.

Activity

Read through our discussion of payment by results systems again and think about the problems which they can generate for management. List three reasons why management may prefer measured daywork. Discuss this with a personnel work study or management services specialist in your organisation if possible.

The advantages you listed are likely to be included among the following:

- the industrial relations problems of payment by results systems are likely to be avoided whilst an incentive element is retained;
- there is a strong sanction against poor performance;
- there should be less resistance to changes in working methods since earnings will not be affected;
- employee cooperation and flexibility should be greater because bonus paid is the same on any job;
- there is greater control over wage costs;
- the system should be cheap to administer since bonus is standard and only the exceptions must be calculated;

- there is a positive incentive to training to maintain bonus earnings.

On the other hand measured daywork requires closer and better supervision than payment by results systems and a steady work flow and effective monitoring of the system. In addition some organisations which have changed from payment by results to measured daywork have experienced at least a short-term fall in productivity.

Plant and organisation-wide incentive schemes, profit sharing and share ownership

The most common of these schemes are:

- **Added value schemes** *Added value = sales revenue less expenditure on materials and services purchased outside the organisation.* Thus, added value is a measure of efficiency. An increase in added value above a given norm represents an improvement in performance which can be shared with employees according to an agreed formula.
- **Profit sharing schemes** These involve the distribution of either cash or shares from company profits in a prespecified way to categories of employees.

In the past there has been a lack of interest in these approaches to payment in the UK.

> *Self-check*
>
> Try to list two reasons for this.

You may have found this difficult unless you have some experience in this area of personnel management. The reasons which have been suggested include:

- employees' difficulty in relating their individual efforts to the amount of bonus received;
- a low level of commitment by workers in the UK to the 'free enterprise society'.

However, there has been an upsurge of interest in these systems recently – particularly in profit sharing, which has been encouraged by government tax concessions.

> *Self-check*
>
> Can you think of any other reasons which might make workplace or enterprise-wide schemes of this kind more popular in future?

Organisations are becoming more capital- rather than labour-intensive and work is becoming more machine-paced. As a result, it is more difficult to design effective payment by results or even measured daywork systems. Yet there will be a need for organisations to be more competitive. Therefore management will continue to search for financial incentives.

Fair benefits at work

So far we have examined methods of monetary remuneration. Before we leave this area of personnel management we must look at non-monetary or 'fringe' benefits.

> *Activity*
>
> Talk to a personnel specialist in your organisation about the range of benefits other than pay which employees receive. List your findings.

Depending on the organisation in which you carried out this activity, your list may have been very long indeed. Some of the items were probably services to employees such as sports and canteen facilities; we discussed these in Chapter 10. Others are likely to have related to the termination of employment and will be covered in Chapter 15.

Other benefits which are sometimes provided include:

- company cars;
- medical and life insurance;
- relocation allowances.

Review

How should management determine its policy on employee benefits?

Management should determine this policy as part of its overall remuneration policy and wage and salary administration practices.

What of the future?

In Chapter 10 we suggested there is a trend to harmonisation in terms and conditions of employment. Some writers predict this may also occur in payment and job evaluation systems as more and more employees are white- rather than blue-collar and as it becomes necessary to justify differences between men and women because of equal pay legislation. Petty and unjustified differences in rewards are likely to offend employees' sense of esteem and achievement. Equity between levels of tasks is vital to generate a sense of fair treatment in pay and benefits.

13 | Managing with trade unions

According to statistics produced by the Department of Employment, over half the working population belongs to a trade union. If we eliminate the self-employed and the armed forces from these figures, we can see that most managers and personnel specialists are likely to be involved with trade union representatives as part of their responsibility for managing groups of employees.

Activity

Interview a line manager or personnel specialist a substantial part of whose role involves dealing with trade unions. Ask him to detail this part of his job for you. Make notes during the interview. From your interview notes list three areas of knowledge and three skills which are needed.

Here is a longer list within which your items are likely to appear:

Knowledge areas
- The structure and organisation of trade unions recognised for collective bargaining purposes and the role of the shop steward.
- The nature of agreements between management and trade unions relevant to the employees for which responsibility is held.
- The nature of the role of the manager or the personnel specialist in industrial relations.
- Employment legislation so far as it affects relationships with trade unions.
- State services in the area of industrial relations such as conciliation and arbitration.

- The influence of factors external to the organisation on industrial relations. An example of this is the nature of demand for the products or services of the organisation and of demand for the labour employed.

Skills
Those involved in industrial relations need general 'people-handling' skills. Some specific examples of these are:

- collective bargaining skills;
- grievance and disciplinary interviewing skills;
- counselling skills;
- skills in working with consultative committees and dealing with representatives where employees participate in managerial decision-making (see Chapter 14).

There are no general prescriptions for the creation of good industrial relations. Therefore managers and personnel specialists can successfully utilise their knowledge and skills only if they are based on a broad understanding of the nature of industrial relations. It is necessary to exercise judgement in the analysis of particular factors which influence industrial relations in the industry or workplace. Therefore neither of the above lists is definitive. In addition a knowledge of policy or senior management's expectations in this area is vital. The largest organisations are generally the most heavily unionised. Here it is necessary for management to coordinate its practices in the industrial relations area. However, even in small organisations it is advisable for all members of management to be fully aware of company policy and practice, if unnecessary conflict with trade unions is to be avoided.

What are industrial relations?

Self-check

Attempt a definition of 'industrial relations'.

It may surprise you to know that there is no one correct definition. You may have said that industrial relations are about the relationship between management and unions. In many cases this is true but what about non-unionised workplaces? It is reasonable to argue that a definition should cover all situations where an employment relationship exists.

A further term which you may have included in your definition to describe the relationship between management and unions is 'collective bargaining' or the means by which rules governing the employment relationship are made. These rules are often classified into two types:

- procedural; and
- substantive.

Procedural rules are those governing the process of industrial relations, or which create a framework within which the parties – management and unions – can negotiate over substantive issues concerning actual terms and conditions of employment such as pay, holidays and fringe benefits.

Self-check

List three types of procedure agreement.

Your items should be covered below:

- disciplinary;
- grievance;
- negotiating;
- disputes;
- redundancy.

Another word which you may have used in your definition of industrial relations is 'conflict'. In the UK we tend to believe that our industrial relations are very strife-torn. Several surveys have shown this not to be the case by indicating that under one per cent of workplaces are affected by strikes in any year. It is more realistic to talk about industrial relations as being about co-operation between management and unions.

Perspectives in industrial relations

From these attempts to define industrial relations you may have gathered that, in this area of organisational decision-making, it is difficult to establish 'the facts'. A key skill in industrial relations, which underlies all the others in our list at the beginning of this chapter, is that of seeing the situation from the other person's perspective. This gives you greater understanding of their position but does not necessarily mean that you will agree with them. Unfortunately many of those involved in dealing with trade unions do not possess this skill; they are 'blinkered' by their own experiences and their own conditioning into believing that theirs is the only valid view.

Self-check

Suggest two ways in which managers and personnel specialists can remove their 'blinkers'.

The answer which may have leapt to mind most readily is 'by training'. Industrial relations training courses can provide a vehicle within which managers can explore their own perceptions of and attitudes to particular industrial relations situations. In a 'safe environment' they can experiment with analysis from a different viewpoint to that which they normally adopt.

A rather less obvious answer is 'through experience'. For example, sometimes full-time trade union officers or senior shop stewards are recruited as personnel specialists. Such people should be able to put themselves in the shoes of trade unionists. However, sometimes the 'poacher turned gamekeeper' is trusted by neither management nor trade unions.

Very often people reveal their perspectives by the words they use. For example, the term 'restrictive practice' is commonly used to describe methods used by workers to limit their flexibility and productivity by illegitimate methods.

Self-check

Suppose you were a member of a work group which wishes to protect its work by refusing to let members of other occupational groups encroach on its territory. What name would you give to a 'restrictive practice'?

You might call it a 'protective practice'. In other words, for you this would be quite legitimate behaviour.

> *Activity*
>
> Look at the interview notes you made earlier on the industrial relations role of a manager or personnel specialist. Did anything which was said reveal the interviewee's perspective?

Your interviewee may have seen conflict as unlikely to arise in the organisation if trade unions were not present and communications were good. In this case, a strong belief in the responsibility of management to manage probably also would have been expressed.

Other managers see trade unions as playing a legitimate and welcome role in representing employees' interests. This is usually accompanied by an acceptance of collective bargaining and a recognition that conflict between management and employees is likely to arise but can be resolved if effective rules govern the relationship between management and unions.

The perspective of your interviewee may not fall neatly into either of these categories. This is because our views of the world often contain contradictions. A relevant example here is the attitude to the closed shop of many managers. On the one hand they are against it as a restriction on the freedom of the individual to join or not to join a trade union. On the other hand they are in favour of it as a means of dealing with all employees through trade union representatives.

Rule-making in industrial relations

Some people believe that the focus of industrial relations is the rules which regulate the relationship between management and trade unions.

> *Self-check*
>
> Some managers see trade unions as playing an important and legitimate role in representing employees' interests.

Does this mean that they would agree that all matters affecting the employment relationship should be subject to negotiation?

No, they would not. Research on this subject has shown that the vast majority of managers are not prepared to negotiate on:

- investment policies;
- pricing policies;
- product and market planning;

and other aspects of overall business planning.

On the other hand, managers frequently are prepared to negotiate on:

- working methods;
- payment methods;
- overtime allocation;
- manning levels;
- disciplinary issues;
- redundancy.

Self-check

Why do you think management generally negotiate about the items on the second list but not those on the first list?

The former items are very much associated with management's overall control of the enterprise, whilst the latter items are day-to-day operational matters which can be agreed with employee representatives without major challenge to the managerial prerogative.

From this we see that not all rules which are the subject matter of industrial relations are made jointly between management and trade unions. Some are made only by management; others are made by workers; yet others are made by the state.

Self-check

What rules are made unilaterally by employees?

Frequently this area of rule-making in industrial relations is known as 'custom and practice', covering:

- overtime;
- mobility of labour;
- entry to apprenticeship (for example, in the printing industry);
- manning levels.

Sometimes lower levels of management 'turn a blind eye' to such practices, thinking it is worth neither time nor potential conflict to eradicate them.

Little of the relationship between management and trade unions is governed by legal statutes. Most employers and trade unionists believe that the law should be seen as a last resort to be used only after negotiations have broken down.

Self-check

Look back to the checklist on employees' legal rights on pp. 174–5 of Chapter 11. We see that individual workers have many legal rights. Do you then agree that industrial relations in the UK have been subject to a minimum of legal intervention?

Since the 1960s individual employees' legal protection from arbitrary managerial action has increased greatly. However, the relationship between employers and trade unions is still subject to little legal regulation.

Self-check

Do you think relations between unions and management would be improved if the law played a greater role?

There is no right answer. It depends on your perspective. Some people say trade unions have too much power and that the law should be used to change this; others argue that trade unions should distrust the judiciary, which has more in common with the 'establishment' and employers than with ordinary working people.

Managerial strategy in industrial relations

> *Self-check*
>
> What are management's objectives in industrial relations?

Management's general objectives are predominantly financial. In industrial relations management is concerned to keep down the costs of employing people whilst at the same time achieving the highest possible productivity. There is the temptation to do what is expedient at the time – in other words, to have no long-term strategy and to take only short-term decisions. This would not be acceptable in other areas of managerial decision-making. Why should industrial relations be treated in this way?

> *Self-check*
>
> In Chapter 8 we examined the training implications of the acquisition by Fred's Food Processing Company of a chain of frozen food shops. Fred's company is unionised. List three decisions about industrial relations strategy which should be made at this time.

The issues for the company which you might have identified are:

- whether to encourage unionisation of the shops, and if so, by what union;
- the level at which collective bargaining should take place – workplace, division (food manufacturing, shops) or company;
- the subjects on which management is prepared to negotiate – pay and other terms and conditions of employment, matters of day-to-day operation or overall business planning;
- whether all employees should be encouraged to join a trade union, or only non-managerial staff;
- whether arrangements for employee consultation should be set up in the shops, and what, if any, should be the involvement of trade union representatives in these. (The subject of employee participation and consulation is covered in Chapter 14.)

The industrial relations implications of corporate decision-making often are examined after financial, production or marketing plans have been made. However, it is more useful to include industrial relations as a facet of general organisational decision-making. Fred could have thought about the implications for employee relations of a decision to expand before he had decided that the best growth strategy was to acquire a chain of frozen food shops. If his food manufacturing company had a history of poor industrial relations, he might have asked himself in what kind of expansion strategy he would be least likely to experience similar problems. The answer might have been in smaller units and in the service rather than the manufacturing sector. This would have given him an industrial relations justification for the option of acquiring a chain of frozen food shops.

Self-check

Why might this decision to acquire the frozen food shops be wise if Fred wishes to avoid industrial relations problems?

The evidence is that small workplaces are less conflict-ridden than large ones. Strikes are less frequent in the private services sector of British industry than in manufacturing. This would not guarantee Fred industrial peace but it would suggest that this could be achieved with goodwill on both sides.

On the other hand, if relations between employees and management in Fred's food manufacturing company were good and productivity was high, Fred might have decided that the least risky expansion strategy, from the industrial relations point of view, would be to open another very similar factory. However, other aspects of the decision – finance and marketing in particular – are likely to be given greater significance than the industrial relations dimension.

Review

Why is this?

This is because of the predominantly financial objectives of work organisations.

Remember that industrial relations and personnel policies are not independent of each other. If the company's expansion does not lead to promotion for those with managerial potential, industrial relations problems from this group may proliferate. Hence an industrial relations strategy must be concerned with employment policies and practices generally and not just with relations between trade unions and management.

It is not only expanding companies which should develop industrial relations strategies. Even in companies with established relations with trade unions, management should assess the industrial relations position periodically and establish whether change in policies or practices is necessary. It is now widely agreed that good industrial relations require foresight, planning and the commitment of top management. Only thus can consistent and effective relationships with trade unions and employees be maintained.

Industrial relations roles in the workplace

Earlier we said that industrial relations is concerned with the employment relationship between management and employees. In this section we consider the roles played by those concerned with the development of this relationship. Procedure agreements define the formal position.

Activity

Examine the procedure agreements used in your workplace. Then list those involved in the resolution of the issues covered by the agreements.

You are likely to have discovered that those involved include:

- various levels of management including supervisors;
- trade union representatives in the workplace;
- personnel and industrial relations specialists.

At higher levels of procedure full-time trade union officers become involved, as do employers' association officials in organisations which belong to such bodies.

However, by no means all interactions between the parties to the employment relationship are played out within the formal framework of procedure agreements. In many workplaces management and trade union representatives have off-the-record discussions during which problems are aired and solutions tested, prior to a more formalised procedural negotiation.

Managerial roles in industrial relations

One of the complications of industrial relations is that different levels and functions of management have different perspectives on, and roles in, this area. Senior management often does not play a front-line role. In this way a bargaining brief can be given to middle or junior management or personnel specialists which does not threaten any fundamental principles and preserves the power and independence of directors and senior management. Sometimes, when negotiations break down, the bargaining position of those who bargain on management's behalf may be over-ridden by their more senior colleagues.

Self-check

What are the dangers of this?

Access to the 'organ-grinder' rather than the 'monkey' may become part of the negotiating process. The resultant demoralisation of management's negotiating team is likely to have a very disadvantageous effect on workplace industrial relations.

The role of personnel specialists

A minority of procedure agreements specify a definite role for the personnel function in workplace industrial relations. The involvement of specialists should increase with the level of conflict because of the need for coordination and specialist knowledge, for example of job analysis, job evaluation and employees' legal rights. Personnel specialists should be concerned with the establishment and maintenance of a good procedural framework for workplace industrial relations which fits management's policy objectives in this area. However, this is difficult since there are often differences of interests between line management and personnel specialists with regard to methods of resolving conflict with trade unions.

> ## Self-check
>
> The computer staff in a bank go on strike over a regrading claim. They have never been on strike before. What do you think their departmental manager will want to do to resolve the issue? Are members of the personnel department likely to agree?

Obviously you need more information to give a carefully thought-out answer. Generally, however, it is likely that the line manager most immediately concerned with the work group will wish to concede the claim to get the service operating again. Personnel specialists, on the other hand, supported by more senior line management, should have an eye on the longer-term issues. There is evidence that if employees come to see strikes or other forms of industrial action as the only way of getting concessions from management, they may use this weapon more and more frequently. Also personnel specialists should be aware of the possible 'knock-on' effect of a regrading of computer staff on other areas of the bank's business.

The personnel specialist may sometimes feel he has a 'piggy in the middle' role in industrial relations, both in terms of the different interest groups within management and as the interface with union representatives, who see the personnel department as the first port of call when there is a problem.

The role of trade union representatives

The most commonly used term for a trade union representative in the workplace is 'shop steward'. Such people have frequently been cast as the villains of industrial relations, particularly by those who see trade unions as introducing conflict into otherwise harmonious working situations. However, there is much evidence that most managers who deal with shop stewards do not so regard them.

A shop steward or trade union representative in the workplace normally:

- is an employee of the organisation;
- is not paid by the trade union;
- spends part of working time on trade union duties;
- is responsible for the representation of members' interests during the initial stages of negotiations with management;
- is often persuaded to take the job because nobody else wants it – though union rules do require election to office.

Activity

Try to talk to a trade union representative. Afterwards, list three aspects of this role.

It includes

- recruitment of members and ensuring that they remain in membership;
- representing members' interests to management;
- giving information on trade union activities and facilities to members.

In most workplaces trade union representatives no longer collect trade union dues. 'Check-off' agreements with management frequently exist so that dues are directly deducted from pay.

Self-check

What effect do you think such agreements may have on workplace trade union organisation?

They reduce the need for frequent contact between members and representatives.

Like that of the personnel specialist, the role of the shop steward lies at an interface between management and employees. This can place contradictory pressures on the representative. In our example from banking in this chapter, the computer staff would expect the representative to get their jobs regraded, whilst personnel specialists would hope that he or she could persuade employees that their grading was correct.

Review

We have examined the nature of workplace industrial relations whilst stressing the difficulty of generalising from one workplace to another. List three lessons for the line manager or the personnel specialist from the discussion here.

The topics you should have included are:

- the need to recognise your own perspective on this area of management and that of the other parties;
- an ability to recognise the need for a strategy which is compatible with the needs of the business, which other members of management understand and to which they are committed;
- the usefulness of training all members of the management team involved in industrial relations;
- the need for managers to be aware of their own limitations in this area and to be prepared to seek specialist help where necessary.

14 | Employee participation in managerial decision-making

Some definitions

'Participation' refers to a situation where employees have the right to some involvement in the decision-making process. There are many ways in which this can occur. In broad terms these can be defined by:

- the level at which decision-making takes place (i.e. from the level of the individual employee's job to board level);
- the extent of the decisions concerned (i.e. whether only a few or many employees are affected);
- the time which it takes for the decision to be implemented (i.e. from day-to-day operational decisions to long-term plans for the future of the organisation).

How does collective bargaining fit into this broad definition? In the UK, as we saw in the last chapter, the subject matter of collective bargaining generally has been confined to wages and other terms and conditions of employment. Thus collective bargaining is a form of participation in a restricted area of managerial decision-making.

A further important point to note from our definition of participation is that employees have 'some involvement' in managerial decision-making. In other words, ultimate control of the organisation remains with management.

It is important to distinguish 'participation' from 'industrial democracy'.

|| *Self-check*

What do you understand by 'industrial democracy'?

This implies some sort of voting system in industrial organisations. As citizens we have a voice in government. As workers we normally have no rights to influence our employer's decisions. Thus, industrial democracy is a more radical concept than participation.

In this chapter we examine management's reasons for seeking to encourage employee participation, together with some of the main methods by which this occurs.

Self-check

Give three reasons why management might choose to involve employees in their decision-making.

You may be interested in the answer of Lord Weinstock, managing director of the General Electric Company. In a memorandum on participation he gave the following reasons for his interest in the subject:

- to improve business performance by developing opportunities for growth and eliminating inefficient practices in the interests of all employees;
- to increase the involvement and commitment of all employees especially at the workplace where they have got the most to give and to gain;
- to ensure proper regard for the dignity of every individual employee.

Other factors which have encouraged management to take an interest in participation over the last two decades include:

- increased union organisation and bargaining strength;
- a better-educated workforce more able and more likely to question managerial decisions;
- more emphasis by unions on the education and training of their representatives;
- the recognition that management does not have a monopoly of skills and capabilities – employees should be encouraged to contribute to decision-making which affects their lives.

In the words of one eminent industrial relations writer, Allan Flanders, 'Management must share control to regain it'.

The power of employees and their trade unions grew during the period of postwar full employment. Employers had to find new ways of containing challenges to their power. By involving employees in managerial decision-making, the threat could be reduced, especially where this resulted in the better understanding of managerial policies and practices by employees. Thus management's main motivation for the introduction of employee participation was economic, and also political in the sense that it was a method of warding off threats to managerial power. It has been concerned with the protection of profits and the pursuit of productivity improvements.

Self-check

If relatively full employment and the consequent increase in union bargaining power were the main reason for increased interest in employee participation, what has been the main reason for a reduction in such interest recently?

Again the reasons are primarily economic. Employee power to challenge managerial prerogatives has declined because of the increased level of unemployment with its consequent effect on the power of trade unions. Hence management has less apparent reason to 'share control to regain it'.

Types of employee involvement

There are many ways in which employees can become involved in managerial decision-making. These can be expressed diagramatically in terms of the degree to which they encroach on the managerial prerogative – see figure 25.

No share in management control

Here the managerial prerogative is absolute. Employees have no right to have their voice heard.

Limited consultation

The UK has a tradition of joint consultation in which manage-

No share in management	Limited consultation with employees	Full consultation with employees	Some share in management	Worker control
1	2	3	4	5

Figure 25. Scale of employee involvement in managerial decision-making

ment has consulted rather than negotiated with employees through committees established for this purpose. Unions have been unhappy with this because of the tendency for management to give information after decisions have been taken. In addition such committees often have had their scope limited to the discussion of 'tea and toilet rolls'. There has been an increase in the number of organisations with such committees over the last decade or so. Only about a third limit employee membership to trade union representatives.

Full consultation

This occurs through committees constituted in the same way as those described above, except that here employees or their representatives are given information on a very broad range of subjects by management. Production, marketing and financial plans as well as personnel matters are discussed. Yet, though mutually acceptable decisions are sought, employees are not able in any way to control managerial decision-making.

> *Activity*
>
> Suppose that Fred has decided to set up a joint consultative committee for the food processing company which he owns. Imagine that you are Fred's personnel officer. List five questions which you would need to answer before establishing the committee.

What are Fred's objectives in establishing the committee? Does he hope that in this way employees may come to understand better the organisation's objectives? Does he want to use the committee as a channel of information to employees? Does he hope to get suggestions from employees which will help him to run the business better? By answering this question you should be able to get some ideas for the terms of reference and constitution of the committee.

What is to be the relationship between the committee and any other bodies? Fred's Food Processing Company is unionised. What is the relationship to be between consultation and collective bargaining?

What is to be the composition of the committee? A decision will need to be made as to whether the employee representation is to be restricted to union representatives. Thought will need to be given as to their numbers and the constituencies from which they are drawn. How many management representatives should there be and how should they be chosen? What about the representation of supervisors? Frequently these people are described as the 'lost men of management'. This can lead to their disaffection with the organisation and sometimes to their unionisation. Who should be the officers of the committee? This may be a role for the personnel officer.

How are the elections for membership of the committee to be organised? Who will organise them? When should they be held? What will be the procedures for nomination of candidates and for voting? Who shall be eligible to stand for election? Can all employees vote?

What should be the detailed arrangements for the operation of the committee? When and where should it meet? Who will prepare the agenda and take the minutes?

Shall the representatives have training to undertake their role? Ideally the answer should be 'yes'. Both management and employee representatives will need fully to understand the role which they have taken on and will need skills both to be effective in committee meetings and to report back to their constituents.

From this we can conclude that, while joint consultation may have a bad reputation in some quarters because of the trivial nature of its subject matter, it can be a very useful communication mechanism if properly organised and used.

Some share in management

Some managers are happy to involve employees up to the second or third stage on our scale. Once this point is exceeded many will feel that their power to control the employment relationship is seriously affected. By contrast, union representatives tend to see consultation as a useful floor from which to achieve greater influence over managerial decision-making. In this way we again see the controversial nature of participation. Collective bargaining has been the traditional method by which unions have achieved some influence over managerial decision-making but only in the limited area of terms and conditions of employment. More recently there has been some attempt by unions to increase the scope of collective bargaining to include aspects of financial, market and production planning. Agreements to negotiate the introduction of new technology with those concerned and to protect them from redundancy have become common.

Other schemes which give workers some share in management are those for the election of worker directors to the boards of organisations. These have mainly been confined to the nationalised industries, though there are a few less publicised schemes in the private sector. The first worker directors were appointed at the British Steel Corporation in 1968. Six out of nineteen members of the BSC board are worker directors. The existence of employee representatives on the board cannot quickly change the relationship between management and employees. However, those in favour of such schemes argue that in the long run this will lead to better relations between management and employees, since decision-making by the board will take account of the employee viewpoint.

Nevertheless, as the evidence to the Bullock Committee* showed, management and unions have many reservations about the election of union representatives to the boards of business

Report of the Committee of Inquiry on Industrial Democracy, Cmnd 6706 HMSO, 1977.

organisations. A changed political climate has seen the abandonment of the worker director experiment at the Post Office because of management opposition, and the ruling out of any elected worker representation during the reorganisation of the National Health Service.

> ## Self-check
>
> List two reasons why management tend to be against worker director schemes. Then list two reasons why trade unions also tend to dislike such schemes.

MANAGEMENT

It is difficult to generalise about every manager. But the reasons given by the Confederation of British Industry in its evidence to the Bullock Committee are some indication of the reasons for management's opposition. These were:

- Worker director schemes involve an irreversible change in company organisation.
- The close harmony needed within a company board would be destroyed.
- Worker directors would become alienated from their fellow employees and this would be damaging to the company.
- There is a need for secrecy in company affairs at this level.

TRADE UNIONS

There is a greater range of views within the trade union movement about the desirability of worker director schemes. The evidence of the Trades Union Congress to the Bullock Committee, for example, was in favour on the grounds that workers should be represented when decisions critical to their interests are discussed at board level. Many unionists are against this method of involvement in managerial decision-making for the following reasons:

- Anxiety that board-level decision-making will conflict with collective bargaining.
- Concern that worker directors may be seduced by the status of

their office into taking a managerial view on issues affecting employees.
- Fear that schemes which give minority representation at board level to employees may be used to stave off more fundamental employee challenges to managerial power.

Much of the pressure for worker directors has come from the European Economic Community but at present there seems little likelihood that the UK will legislate for such changes.

Worker control

Here employees totally control the organisation often through a worker cooperative. They hire managers to implement their decisions. Profits are shared by the employees.

Generally in the UK over recent years worker cooperatives have been set up by employees anxious to protect their livelihoods when their employing organisation has foundered. Many of them, such as the *Scottish Daily News*, Kirkby Manufacturing & Engineering and Triumph Motorcyles at Meriden, subsequently failed.

‖ *Self-check*

‖ Does this indicate that workers are unable to run their own
‖ businesses?

This is a matter of opinion. I think it would be unfair to reach this conclusion on the basis of evidence from organisations which were only sold to workers because their owners had been unable to make a profit!

In a few cases organisations have been given to employees through the idealism of the owner. Scott Bader, a small chemicals manufacturer, is an example.

Direct or indirect participation

Our discussion of the ways in which employees can be involved in managerial decision-making has centred on participation through employee representatives, or indirect participation. Some people argue that employees have vague ideas that they would like more information on management's plans but no strong desire to participate in top management decision-making. However, they do seem to want more involvement in matters related to their own jobs. This is the argument for direct participation.

Review

In Chapter 6 we looked at methods of direct participation. Name three of these.

ANSWER

- Quality circles.
- Suggestion schemes.
- Autonomous work groups.

The challenge for management

At the simplest level management is a more straightforward process when workers have no share in organisation decision-making. So far as the management of people is concerned, the job of the manager is to tell employees what they are required to do and ensure that they do it. All planning, control and other managerial activities rests solely with management. When workers participate in managerial decision-making, managers must have the necessary information and skills to carry out organisational policy in this area. (See figure 26.)

From this we see that decisions about employee involvement should not be taken without careful analysis of the implications for managerial jobs. This should be followed by an assessment as to whether managers can cope with subsequent changes in their roles. In general such changes require managers to be more flexible. A more detailed analysis of the new skill requirements is likely to show the need for the following:

- improved communication skills;

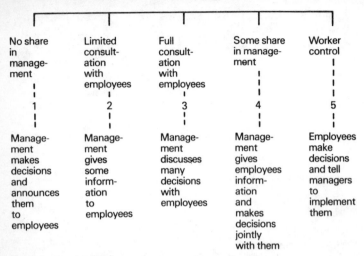

Figure 26. Implications of employee participation for managerial skills and style

- improved written and oral presentation skills;
- improved interpersonal skills especially in working with groups.

As we have seen, most participatory schemes are of the indirect representational type. Managers will need skills to cope with this similar to those used in collective bargaining. However the 'win–lose' tactics often used in collective bargaining are not appropriate here. The skills involved are those of joint decision-making and problem-solving.

15 | Dismissal, redundancy and retirement

Dismissal – an introduction

It is vital that managers handle problem employees very carefully such that accusations of unfair dismissal are unlikely to be upheld if the employee's contract is subsequently terminated. In this section we shall examine the constructive handling of employees in cases where disciplinary action is necessary as well as the law relating to dismissal.

The legal processes for dealing with dismissal cases are identical to those which are used to deal with employee complaints about employers' behaviour with regard to other aspects of the contract of employment.

To stimulate your thinking about discipline and dismissal, I have drawn up some questions for you to attempt to answer here. At the end of the section you will find some similar questions. If the chapter has succeeded in increasing your knowledge of this subject you should find it easier to answer the second set.

Self-check

Comment on the degree to which the following statements are correct.

1 Employees must be given at least one warning before they can be fairly dismissed.
2 All employees can bring claims of unfair dismissal against their employer if they are dismissed.
3 An employee only has the right to be represented at a disciplinary interview when the final warning stage has been reached.

4 An employee who has been found guilty of a shop-lifting offence may be dismissed.
5 Employees have so many legal rights now that it is very difficult to dismiss them.
6 A rent collector, employed by a local authority, who 'borrows' his rent money may be dismissed.

In attempting to answer these questions you probably found that you not only needed a knowledge of the law but also information on the procedures for dealing with disciplinary cases in the organisation concerned. Here are some brief answers to the questions. The actions which managers should take in such circumstances are covered in more detail later in this section.

ANSWERS

1 There were two main points which you could have covered here. First, guidance on the processes to be followed prior to dismissal should be·found in the organisation's disciplinary procedure. Secondly, employees can be dismissed immediately if they commit 'gross misconduct'. There is no universal definition of this term. Again the relevant reference document is the disciplinary procedure.
2 Not all employees can bring such claims against their employer. We shall examine this area of the law on unfair dismissal later in this section.
3 This is incorrect. According to the ACAS Code of Practice on *Disciplinary Practice and Procedures in Employment*, employees have a general right to be accompanied by a trade union representative or by a fellow employee. Whether this means that the latter can speak on behalf of the 'accused' is usually defined in the organisation's disciplinary procedure.
4 Whether or not a tribunal would find dismissal to be fair in this case would depend largely on the nature of the employee's job. Those expected to be trustworthy and of great integrity, such as security guards or cashiers, tend to be treated differently from junior clerical staff, for example.
5 It is not very difficult to dismiss employees fairly if procedures are followed and justice is seen to be done.

6 Most disciplinary procedures would make it clear that this is gross misconduct. Dismissal would be justified provided that the employee's action could be proved beyond reasonable doubt.

From your prior knowledge of the law you probably will have answered some of these questions correctly. The answers may have clarified some of your uncertainties. In the section which follows you should be able to fill in other gaps in your knowledge.

Self-check

From the answers listed above identify three things which managers or personnel specialists need to know in order to be able to deal effectively with disciplinary matters and dismissal.

ANSWER

- Most obviously a knowledge of the law is required.
- Disciplinary procedures are a second source of guidance.
- An awareness of the way that similar cases have been dealt with is necessary. Personnel specialists usually play a co-ordinating and advisory role here.

You may also have suggested that managers and specialists need skills in dealing with these cases. Before we undertake a more detailed examination of the law and of disciplinary procedures we turn to this.

Discipline handling skills

My dictionary defines the verb *to discipline* as 'to bring under control' or 'to train to obedience and order'. In the work situation there is usually an attempt to modify the offending employee's behaviour so that it more closely accords with the management's requirements. Whilst the possibility of sanctions is ever present, the focus is often on problem-solving.

Self-check

List two reasons for the use of an interview as the medium for reprimanding employees.

ANSWER

- In most cases management wishes to help the employee to overcome his difficulties. It is hard to envisage how this can be achieved effectively other than face to face.
- It is important that the employee is given an opportunity to explain his case. In law this is vital if a subsequent dismissal is to be considered fair.

A further point is that management will wish to try to ensure that the malaise does not spread to other staff. Justice must not only be done; it must be seen to be done.

Preparation for disciplinary interviewing

Activity

One of your subordinates, eighteen-year-old Sarah Green, is giving you cause for concern. She is often late for work, takes long lunch hours and occasionally takes odd days off without permission. Her work contains mistakes and she is resistant to suggestions that she should be more careful.

List four types of information which you would need before conducting a disciplinary interview.

You would need knowledge of the following:

- The job – nature of the duties and of the standard of work required.
- The working environment – what are the physical conditions of her job? What are the working relationships?
- Sarah's work record and circumstances – do you have information on her past performance and behaviour?
- Sarah's misdemeanours – when has she been late and how often? When has she been away from work without permission? What inadequacies are there in her job performance?

Having established the facts of the situation, you must also acquaint yourself with the possible sanctions available to you. Only with adequate preparation will you be able to conduct a constructive interview with Sarah.

Participants in disciplinary interviews

Managers will need to consider whether they wish to conduct disciplinary interviews alone or with the help of personnel specialists. Some procedure agreements specify the point at which the latter should become involved. If such guidance is not available then it will be necessary for the management to consider the degree of formality which is useful in the circumstances.

As we saw at the beginning of this section, employees have the right to be accompanied either by a union representative or by a colleague in these situations. To safeguard themselves from later accusations of unfairness, managers would be best advised to inform employees of this right. The presence of a union representative should not be feared. Very often this acts as additional insurance that promises made by employees of future improvements in behaviour or performance will be carried out.

The interview itself

The initiative for the interview comes from management. Firstly there should be an attempt to establish the full facts both by explaining what information is held and by asking for the employee's comments. Forcing a confession by attempting to place the individual under considerable stress or preaching a sermon is unlikely to contribute to the correction of the problem. A more constructive approach is to try to agree with the employee how improvement can be achieved. Such a problem-solving approach will be assisted by the judicious use of questions.

Self-check

Refer back to the categories of questions which we used in our discussion of the selection interview in Chapter 3, pp. 52–4. List two categories which are likely to be useful in a constructive disciplinary interview.

The most obvious are open and probing questions to establish the employee's perception of the situation. Linking statements or questions should also be used to ensure that the interview is a conversation with a purpose. Indirect questions may be useful in further assisting your understanding.

Follow-up of disciplinary interviews

It is important to keep an accurate record of the interview, both to ensure that agreements are kept and in case the situation is not rectified and the employee is subsequently dismissed. New facts which have come to light during the interview must be checked. For example, if Sarah complained that a contributory factor to her poor performance was constant interruption from workmates, this would need to be verified. The employee's subsequent behaviour and performance must be carefully monitored to determine whether further disciplinary action is necessary.

Disciplinary procedures

Employers must give employees details of any disciplinary rules applicable to them and the name of someone to whom appeal can be made against a disciplinary decision as part of the written particulars of the contract of employment. The law does not require organisations to have disciplinary rules or procedures. However, as we shall see, employers who act unfairly in disciplining employees are likely to face adverse tribunal decisions if dismissed employees seek legal redress. The ground rules on fairness are set out in the code of practice on *Disciplinary Practices and Procedures in Employment* issued by ACAS. Wise employers have incorporated these into their own procedures and practices. Though infringements of the code are not of themselves actionable offences, the absence of procedures or their breach is likely to make it difficult for the employer to argue before a tribunal that he acted fairly. However, account will be taken of the circumstances of the case.

Essential features of a disciplinary procedure The ACAS Code of Practice says that disciplinary procedures should:

- be in writing;
- specify to whom they apply;
- provide for matters to be dealt with quickly;
- indicate the disciplinary action which may be taken;
- specify the levels of management which have the authority to take the various forms of disciplinary action. Immediate superiors do not normally have the power to dismiss without reference to senior management;
- provide for individuals to be informed of the complaints against them and to be given an opportunity to state their case before decisions are reached;
- give individuals the right to be accompanied by a trade union representative or by a fellow employee of their choice;
- ensure that, except for gross misconduct, no employees are dismissed for a first breach of discipline;
- ensure that disciplinary action is not taken until the case has been carefully investigated;
- ensure that individuals are given an explanation for any penalties imposed;
- provide a right of appeal and specify the procedure to be followed.

The Code also suggests that if, after investigation, it is found that formal action should be taken against the employee the following stages should be followed:

- in the case of minor offences, the employee should be given a formal oral warning or, if the issue is more serious, there should be a written warning and the employee should be advised that the warning constitutes the first formal stage of the procedure;
- further misconduct might warrant a final written warning;
- the final step might be disciplinary transfer or suspension without pay (but only if these are allowed for by an express or implied term of the contract of employment) or dismissal.

Self-check

Look back to the case of Sarah Green. Assume that you are her immediate superior and that the organisation has a speedy written procedure agreement which specifies that offences such as those which she has committed are minor (as opposed to those for which summary dismissal is permissible). Identify four areas of guidance in the extracts from the ACAS Code of Practice which you should observe in dealing with Sarah.

You should:

- inform her of what you believe to be the case against her and give her the opportunity to state her case;
- ask her if she wishes her trade union representative or a friend to be present while you talk to her;
- carefully investigate the case before disciplinary action is taken;
- ensure that you explore the options carefully before taking action against her; in this case the choice will be either an oral or a first written warning.

You would also be advised to ensure, if you take action, that she understands the reason for the imposition of a penalty, the next stage of procedure which will be used if matters do not improve and her rights of appeal, if any, at this stage.

Trade unions and disciplinary procedures

An important part of the trade union representative's role where unions are recognised is the representation of members who are subject to disciplinary action. As we have seen, the ACAS Code of Practice emphasises the legitimacy of this. Many disciplinary procedures have been jointly agreed with trade unions, who generally see them as a means of ensuring the equitable treatment of employees. When it comes to disciplinary rules trade unions are likely to be less willing to share control with management. Many trade unionists argue that it is vital to maintain flexibility here in order to protect members' interests.

Care should be taken if it becomes necessary to discipline a trade union representative, since this could be seen as an attack on the union. The Code of Practice suggests that no formal action should be taken until the matter has been discussed with either a full-time union official or with a more senior representative.

The law on dismissal

Observance of the guidance in the earlier part of this chapter should be both helpful in the maintenance of good employee relations, and supportive of the employer's case should subsequent dismissal lead to a tribunal hearing. To deal effectively with dismissal, managers and personnel specialists also need a good knowledge of the law. This is contained mainly within the Employment Protection Consolidation Act 1978, though there were minor amendments in the Employment Act 1980.

What is dismissal?

According to the law, employees are treated as dismissed if:

- the contract of employment under which they work is terminated by the employer with or without notice;
- a fixed-term contract expires without being renewed;
- they leave their employment 'in circumstances such that [they are]entitled to terminate it without notice by reason of the employer's conduct' – constructive dismissal.

Constructive dismissal This occurs when management puts pressure on the employee to resign in a way which goes to the root of the contract. The most obvious example is where management materially changes the contract of employment without the employee's consent.

Self-check

You are the owner of a chain of five hairdressing salons. Jane Jones is a stylist at one of them. You tell her that in a month's time she will work at another one. Is this constructive dismissal?

To decide this it would be necessary to examine Jane's contract of employment and the effect on it of your conduct. If the contract says that she has been employed as a stylist at any of your shops and it is customary for staff to move around in this way, then you may be in the clear. By contrast if the contract states that the location of her employment is the salon in which she is currently working, she has worked there for a long time and stylists are never expected to move, then your case will be very weak.

In order to make a claim of constructive dismissal against you she must leave without notice. Your best protection against such claims is to get her agreement to the move.

Who can claim unfair dismissal?

Review

Remembering the checklist of employee rights in Chapter 11, pp. 174–5, list three categories of employees who cannot make claims of unfair dismissal.

ANSWER

- Those with less than one year's service.
- Those with less than five years' service who work more than eight and less than sixteen hours a week.
- Those with less than two years' service who work for an employer who has twenty or less employees.

Employees who 'normally' work abroad, those over normal retirement age and those employed by a spouse are among those also excluded from bringing unfair dismissal cases.

What is fair and unfair dismissal?

Once it has been established that a dismissal has taken place, the employer must prove that the employee was dismissed for one of the potentially fair reasons laid down in law. These reasons concern issues of:

- capability or qualifications for the work which the employee must do;
- conduct;
- redundancy;
- where continuing to employ the worker would be illegal;
- some other substantial reason.

However, showing that the employee was dismissed for a fair reason is not sufficient. The employer must also be able to prove that the punishment – the dismissal – fitted the crime. If the employer fails to show the reason or shows a reason which is not listed above, then the dismissal will be automatically unfair. If a valid reason is shown, then the employer must show that it was reasonable to dismiss the employee in the circumstances. Tribunals will pay careful attention to the facts of the particular case.

The law has different standards for small and large businesses. Small firms are treated more leniently, for example, for failing to use fair procedures or failing to offer alternative work to employees who become unable to cope with the demands of their jobs.

Now we examine the general approach of the courts and tribunals to dismissal for the five potentially valid reasons listed above.

Capability or qualifications This covers employee incompetence (intentional or unintentional), short- and long-term sickness and lack of qualifications to do the job.

If an employee falls below expected standards of performance, management must show that the reasons for the decline have been investigated, warnings have been given and attempts have been made to help the employee to improve. Whether or not it is necessary to offer alternative work will depend on the size of the organisation and the length of service of the employee.

Similar considerations will apply where employees' poor health makes them incapable of coping with the demands of their job. The law on dismissal due to long-term sickness is particularly complex. Obviously warnings that a failure to return to work will result in dismissal would be inappropriate! Employers are expected to be sympathetic and hold the job open as long as is reasonably practicable. Tribunals will attempt to balance the employer's need for the work to be done against the employee's need to make a proper recovery from his illness.

In cases of short-term absence warnings of the necessity to improve attendance should be given, though again the circumstances must be investigated. Medical certificates can be requested even for single days of absence. In making a decision to dismiss, it is legitimate to take into account the disruptive effect of repeated short spells of absence on the efficiency of the organisation.

The cases on lack of qualification are few since this must be a condition of employment. Most people who lack adequate qualifications are not selected in the first place. An example would be where a trainee fails to pass examinations without which he cannot practise. Even then it might be reasonable for the employer to extend the training period.

Conduct This term is not defined in the legislation and an examination of cases indicates that a wide range of misconduct has been said to justify dismissal. If an offence is accepted to be gross misconduct then dismissal without notice would be an appropriate sanction. For less serious cases, warnings would be necessary prior to dismissal. In these cases it is vital that procedures are followed and that employees who breach disciplinary rules are treated equitably.

> ### Self-check
>
> Sarah Green is summarily dismissed for her persistent lateness, long lunch hours and occasional days of absence without permission. Would a tribunal be likely to find the dismissal fair?

The answer must be 'no', since this would not be gross misconduct.

Redundancy Here we are concerned with whether the employer acted reasonably in selecting employees for redundancy. The courts have laid down principles of good practice which employers would be advised to follow in appropriate circumstances:

- As much warning as possible should be given of impending redundancies so that employers and unions together can seek alternative solutions or other work for those involved.
- Unions should be consulted so that management can achieve its objective with the minimum of hardship.

- Criteria for selection should not depend only on the judgement of the person making the selection. They should be objective and related to attendance, experience, efficiency and length of service. Where possible they should be agreed with trade unions.
- Selection should be on the basis of these criteria.
- Management should investigate the possibilities of alternative employment for those involved.

In addition it would be unfair to select employees for redundancy on grounds of either trade union membership or non-membership.

Self-check

In a redundancy situation, the management of Len's Lorries decide that those employees with the shortest service must go first. Is this selection criterion likely to be accepted as fair by the courts?

If Len's Lorries made an agreement to this effect with a recognised trade union, the answer is likely to be 'yes'. If not, the test would be whether this was a reasonable and objective criterion. In most circumstances this would be agreed to be the case.

Legal restrictions An employer may fairly dismiss an employee whose continued employment would be against the law. This covers such cases as drivers who become disqualified from driving, or employees who do not have a work permit.

Some other substantial reason This last 'catch-all' category has been used to cover reductions in wages or changes in hours of work which are argued by the employer to be vital if the business is to survive, the dismissal of temporary employees who have been employed to replace staff absent because of medical suspension or maternity leave, and irreconcilable conflicts between employees where the dismissed employee can be shown to be the main instigator of the trouble.

Reasons for dismissal which are automatically unfair

These are:

- dismissal for being a member of or taking part in the activities of an independent trade union;
- dismissal because of race or sex discrimination;
- dismissal because of pregnancy, unless the employer can show that the woman concerned is no longer capable of doing the work she was employed to do.

The dismissal of strikers is not automatically unfair provided that none of them are re-engaged within six months of the dismissal. Neither is it automatically unfair to dismiss those who refuse to join a trade union where a closed shop exists, though in this case there are major exceptions.

Remedies for unfair dismissal

Employees who successfully bring a claim of unfair dismissal against their employers are entitled to remedies in this order:

- reinstatement;
- re-engagement;
- compensation.

Reinstatement If the tribunal orders reinstatement, management must treat the employee as if the employment had not been terminated.

> *Self-check*
>
> List four factors to be taken into account when reinstating a dismissed employee.

ANSWER

- Back-pay including any pay increases which should have been received.
- The need to preserve the dismissed employee's continuity of service.
- Any benefits to which the dismissed employee is entitled –

holiday pay, for example.
- The date by which the tribunal's order for reinstatement is to be complied with.

Tribunals seldom order reinstatement. In making such decisions they take account of the employee's wishes, the practicality of such an order for management and the degree to which the employee contributed to his own dismissal.

Re-engagement In this case the employee must be re-employed but not necessarily in the same job. Again the cases in which tribunals make such an order are relatively few and the same factors are taken account of as for reinstatement.

Compensation This is awarded if management is not ordered to re-employ the dismissed employee or if such an order is ignored. There are four types of compensation:

- the basic award – equivalent to a redundancy payment;
- the compensatory award – based on an assessment of what the employee has lost in wages, benefits, etc. now and in the future;
- the additional award – if management do not comply with an order for reinstatement or re-engagement;
- the special award – in cases of dismissal for union membership or non-membership.

Both the basic award and the compensatory award will be reduced if the tribunal believes that the employee contributed to his dismissal. The compensatory award is reduced also if the employee failed to attempt to compensate for the loss of the job.

Dismissed workers are also entitled to a written statement of the reasons for dismissal. If this has not been given a tribunal can order additional compensation of up to two weeks' pay.

Review

From your knowledge of discipline and dismissal now, comment on the degree to which these statements are correct.

1 One of the employees you supervise resigned last week. You didn't like him and are relieved that he's left. You have nothing further to worry about.
2 If employees are persistently late you can dismiss them summarily.
3 You discipline a trade union representative for persistent lateness. Because of his position you should consult a full-time union official or senior representative.
4 A local authority manager required to drive a car as part of his job loses his driving licence for a year. He says that his wife will drive him around while he is disqualified. You say that this is unacceptable and dismiss him.
5 A secretary complains to a personnel officer that her boss continually swears at her. The personnel officer thinks that she is a bit of a prude and takes no action.

ANSWERS

1 Depending on the circumstances of the case this might be constructive dismissal.
2 Since this would not be gross misconduct such dismissals would be unfair.
3 The action in this case conforms with the ACAS Code of Practice.
4 Dismissal because it would be illegal to continue to employ him is unlikely to be fair in this case, though it would depend on the particular requirements of the job. The local authority would be expected to find some other way of enabling him to cope with the demands of his job. However, it would not be expected to come to an arrangement with his wife!
5 It would be wise to investigate this complaint, since if it goes to the 'root of the contract' it might be construed as constructive dismissal.

Redundancy

This is probably the saddest and most difficult problem of the employment relationship with which managers and personnel specialists have to deal.

Activity

Redundancy has become commonplace in our society. The odds are that you know someone who has been involved in such a situation. Ask them to describe the situation to you. Afterwards identify three important considerations for management once it became apparent that redundancy is inevitable.

The considerations you may have listed include:

- who to make redundant, in which areas of the business and on what date or dates;
- whether retraining of redundant employees would be in the interests of the organisation;
- what compensation should be awarded to those made redundant.

It is necessary for managers to think about these issues whatever the detailed circumstances. In unionised organisations it will also be vital to draw up a programme for consulting the unions. This may or may not involve the negotiation of a procedure for handling the redundancies, if such an agreement does not already exist. Sometimes management takes steps to assist redundant employees to find other work. Most often this occurs where the effect of the loss of jobs on the local community is likely to be severe. In these situations most attention tends to be given to the process of identifying and dealing with those who are to be made redundant. However, it is also sensible to consider those who will remain. The shock of redundancy, especially of large numbers of employees, affects future relationships between management and workers.

Review

Remembering the checklist in Chapter 11, pp. 174–5, who can make a claim of redundancy against their employer?

The most obvious category is those with two years' service or more (five years for those working between eight and sixteen hours a week). In addition workers must have been dismissed before they can make a claim. The legal definition of dismissal on p. 247 applies to dismissals because of redundancy. Redundant workers may bring claims for unfair dismissal, as we saw on pp. 250–1. In this section we examine employeecs' rights to redundancy compensation as distinct from compensation for unfair dismissal.

Situations of redundancy

The definition of redundancy covers three main situations:

- where the business ceases to operate;
- where the employer changes the location of the business;
- where the employer requires fewer employees for the existing work.

The first of these categories has given rise to few problems in the courts.

If management wishes to move to another place, the question as to whether workers are redundant will depend on the details of the contract of employment. If this does not require them to move, then they will be able to claim redundancy compensation.

The most controversial redundancy cases have arisen where management decides that there is less work for employees to do or that the same work can be done by fewer people. In such cases work may be reorganised and technology may be changed with consequent implications for the terms and conditions of employment under which people are employed. The courts have upheld management's right to reorganise work in the interests of efficiency. In doing so they have argued that redundancy arises only if there is a change in terms and conditions of employment because the employer's need for 'work of a particular kind' has 'ceased' or 'diminished'. Similarly where the requirement for overtime is reduced, employees are not redundant if management still requires them to do their work as before.

Sometimes the reorganisation of work or change in technology places new demands on employees for efficiency or adaptability. The decisions of the courts in these cases sometimes seem harsh. Take, for example, the case of the woman who had eighteen years' service as a bar-tender. A new manager decided to glamorise the pub and employ 'young blondes and bunny girls'.

Because 'her kind' of bar-tender was no longer required, she was sacked and claimed redundancy pay.

> *Self-check*
>
> According to the definitions of redundancy given on p. 256, do you think that the bar-tender was redundant?

When this case came to the High Court it was argued that there was still a need for bar-tenders, and that therefore she was not redundant. She had become unsuitable for the demands of the job. You may feel, as I do, that this was an unjust decision. Certainly the lay members of the tribunal found in her favour. In any case this decision was made in the days prior to the passing of the legislation on unfair dismissal. Had she been able to bring such a claim, the decision might have been different.

Selection of employees for redundancy

The selection of those employees who must leave can be very painful. We looked at the legal restrictions on this in the last section. Very often selection criteria are agreed with trade unions either at the time of redundancy or when redundancy is only a small dark cloud in an otherwise clear sky.

Redundancy is a difficult issue for trade unions. The views of the members are often divided; some will want to leave with the best possible compensation; others will believe that the union should fight all job losses. However, as redundancy has become more common, trade union opposition has been reduced both by legal rights to compensation and to be consulted and by the weakening of worker power as the dole queues have lengthened. In unionised workplaces there is likely to be a demand that volunteers should be allowed to go first.

> *Self-check*
>
> What are the disadvantages of this from management's point of view?

Those who volunteer are likely to include some people who

would find it easy to get other jobs, people whose skills management would wish to retain. The problem for management of accepting this process of self-selection is that it means surrendering control to workers.

Self-check

In a redundancy situation which workers do you think management would wish to make redundant?

Those who make the smallest contribution to the efficiency of the organisation – the 'slackers', the 'passengers', the 'deadwood', etc. This is where many managers and personnel specialists face something of a crisis of conscience, for these people in all probability will be those who will have the greatest difficulty in getting other jobs. In such situations 'last in first out' may seem to be a fairer criterion. Sometimes criteria are formalised in a redundancy procedure agreement but often management are reluctant to restrict their flexibility to act in this way.

Legally, employers must *consult* recognised independent unions about every proposed redundancy. All employees are covered apart from short-term workers employed for a period of three months or less. The law does not say that there must be negotiation with the unions. 'Consultation' involves giving, in writing, to the union:

- the reasons for the proposals of redundancy;
- the numbers and description (i.e. jobs) of the employees;
- the total number of employees in those jobs;
- the proposed method of selecting employees for redundancy;
- the proposed method of carrying out the redundancies – timing, methods of payment, etc.

After this, management must consider the union's views and must reply to them, stating the reasons for rejecting any of them.

The law says that consultation over any redundancies must begin 'at the earliest opportunity'. When large numbers of redundancies are proposed, the following timetable must be observed at the minimum:

- If 100 employees are to be made redundant at one establishment over a period of up to ninety days, the consultation must take place at least ninety days before the first dismissal takes place.

- If between 10 and 100 workers are to be made redundant at one establishment over a period of up to thirty days, then consultation must take place at least thirty days before the first dismissal takes place.

If management does not observe this timetable, employees made redundant are entitled to additional compensation. This consists of payment for the 'protected period', i.e. the ninety or thirty days specified for the above categories. Tribunals reduce this amount by earnings or payments in lieu of notice paid during this period.

The Department of Employment must also be notified in writing using a similar timetable. Employers are entitled to a rebate from a national fund in respect of statutory redundancy payments. Failure to give the necessary notice to the Department of Employment can result in a reduction in the rebate.

Retraining or redeployment of redundant workers

Another option for management, if the need for workers is reduced, is to consider the possibility of retraining for other work in the organisation or elsewhere. In addition some workers may be able to be redeployed without further training.

Retraining for work elsewhere can be an expensive option, especially when unemployment is high or where workers' skills are obsolete. Some organisations offer counselling services to redundant employees to demonstrate their concern, relieve anxieties and enhance the reputation of the organisation as an employer in the long run.

The speed of technical change tends to mean that adaptation to the demands of new jobs will be a permanent feature of employment. The need for a flexible labour force should add emphasis to the need for manpower planning to identify areas of redundant skills in order that the viability of retraining can be thoroughly investigated.

It may be possible to offer some redundant employees new

jobs immediately. In law if employees accept 'suitable alternative work' they are not entitled to redundancy compensation. For such offers of work to be suitable the following conditions must be met:

- the offer must be made before the old contract is terminated and must take effect within four weeks;
- the offer must be made by the old employer, by management of the same group of companies or by a new employer who is taking over the business;
- the offer can be made orally or in writing and must give the employee information about 'capacity and place . . . and . . . other terms and conditions of employment';
- sufficient information must be given to enable the employee to make a decision as to the suitability of the new job.

If the employee refuses alternative work which is suitable, the right to redundancy compensation is forfeited. In making decisions as to suitability, the tribunal takes account of the employee's personal circumstances including travel, housing, domestic problems or loss of friends.

Self-check

A secretary works for a fashion business in Mayfair, London. The firm moves to new premises above a sex shop in Soho. She refuses the offer of alternative employment there on the grounds that she is opposed to 'money-for-sex' activities and finds the new place of employment distasteful. Is her refusal of the new job unreasonable?

The industrial tribunal said it was and refused her application for a redundancy payment. They said that her refusal to work near a sex shop was based on a personal whim since the commercial exploitation of sex was no greater in Soho than in Mayfair. Possibly it was a little more discrete in the latter area! In this case it was felt that the employee's personal circumstances did not make the refusal of the offer of alternative work reasonable.

Employees who are offered a new job have the right to try it for a period of four weeks. During this period they can leave at any time and claim redundancy compensation. It is then up to the tribunal to decide whether the new job was suitable and whether its rejection was reasonable.

Redundancy compensation

Scales of minimum compensation in cases of redundancy are laid down by law. The amount of the payment depends on the employee's age, length of service and weekly pay. Only those who have two or more years' service have a legal entitlement to be compensated in this way. Many organisations have paid more to redundant workers than the statutory minimum. Employees have the right to a written statement from management explaining how the compensation has been calculated.

Review

Look back to the checklist in Chapter 11. Redundant workers have a further legal right which so far has not been discussed in this chapter. What is it?

This is the right to 'reasonable' paid time off to look for other work or for retraining whilst under notice of redundancy. This is only available to workers with at least two years' service. Even if employees are offered alternative work, they are entitled to this. There is no legal definition of what is reasonable. It would depend on the circumstances such as the amount of work available and the time and travel involved in looking for it. In practice the amount of time off given tends to be rather limited. If management refuses to allow employees this right, the maximum compensation which can be awarded by a tribunal is two days.

Those who remain after a redundancy

In redundancy, most attention is focused on the plight of those who must leave. Management should not forget those who will continue to be employed. The announcement of redundancy, especially if large numbers of people are involved, usually sends tremors throughout the organisation. Those who stay may feel that their employment with the organisation is no longer permanent and that their career prospects have been affected adversely. Management must systematically assess the nature of these changes and immediately should set about the rebuilding process in ways which convince remaining employees that they have a future.

Review

The implication of our discussion has been that on occasions it is inevitable that employees will be redundant. But is redundancy inevitable? Look back to Chapter 2 and then list three things which can be done to avoid redundancy.

The general answer is that manpower planning should alert the organisation to the possibility of redundancy. Then the need to shed labour can be reduced or avoided altogether by some of the following measures:

- stopping recruitment;
- halting overtime;
- encouraging early retirement;
- introducing job-sharing;
- developing retraining programmes.

Retirement

The normal retirement age is sixty-five for men and sixty for women. However, as we have seen, early retirement has become much more prevalent as many organisations have slimmed down their labour forces. In this section we shall look at the process of retirement and in particular at pension schemes. Relevant areas of the law will also be examined.

Pension schemes

This is a complex subject on which managers and personnel specialists require specialist advice from actuaries and investment advisers. Here we are only scratching the surface.

The state pension scheme

This is a two-tier scheme which consists of a basic flat-rate retirement pension and an additional earnings-related pension. An employer may contract out of the latter part of the state scheme if he provides an occupational pension scheme which provides benefits which are as good as or better than the state scheme.

Occupational pension schemes

Pensions are probably the most important employee benefit after basic pay.

Self-check

Why should an organisation provide the best possible occupational pension scheme for its employees? List three reasons.

ANSWER

- It helps the recruitment and retention of employees, especially more senior and older employees.
- It is a demonstration that the organisation is a good employer; this should assist the commitment of employees.
- Most employers feel that those who retire should be able to enjoy financial security in their later years.

Contributory and non-contributory occupational pension schemes Most pension schemes require employees to contribute part of their earnings – usually 6 or 7 per cent – to the pension fund from which they will later receive a pension. These are contributory schemes. In this sense pensions are a form of deferred earnings. Other schemes are non-contributory in that their full cost is paid by the employer.

Self-check

Identify one advantage of contributory pension schemes and one of non-contributory schemes.

Contributory schemes generally can provide a better range of benefits because more money is available. Also employees are often more appreciative of benefits for which they have paid.

By contrast non-contributory schemes are often cheaper to administer, are flexible and very attractive to employees since no deductions are made from pay. Trade unions are generally not in favour of non-contributory schemes since they may act as 'golden chains' which tie employees to the organisation because benefits are forfeited on leaving.

Who is covered? It is common to find schemes which cover both staff and manual workers; however, senior management often have a 'top-hat' arrangement. This frequently means that for them the scheme is topped up with a non-contributory arrangement.

Benefits The most obvious benefit is a pension on retirement.

Activity

Find out what other benefits are provided by the pension scheme of which you are a member. If you are not in work or are not old enough to belong to your employer's pension scheme, ask someone who is covered by such an arrangement. (Usually employees do not join pension schemes until they are twenty-one or twenty-five and have six months' service.)

The most usual benefits are:

- a lump sum on retirement;
- death-in-service benefit;
- pension for widows or widowers.

In addition pension schemes can be more or less inflation-proofed by allowing for increases in the pensions paid to those who have retired in response to changes in the cost of living. This is a very desirable feature, although it can be expensive.

Provisions for early retirement

One of the ways of avoiding compulsory redundancy is for

employees nearing retirement age to retire early. Many organisations also allow employees in poor health to leave early. Pension schemes have rules to cope with this eventuality. Normally such people can draw a pension immediately but as their contributions will have been less than those who retire normally, their pension will be smaller. Some employers are generous in the pensions which are paid to older workers who retire at a time of redundancy. Lump-sum payments may also be made.

Provisions for late retirement

Sometimes employers want to retain the services of some employees beyond retirement age. The rules of pension schemes usually provide for such people to receive an enhanced pension without further contributions either from them or from the employer.

Review

List two advantages of early retirement for redundant employees and two advantages of the use of this option as a method of coping with redundancy for management.

ADVANTAGES FOR REDUNDANT EMPLOYEES

- A basic income is provided which can be supplemented by other earnings if other work can be found.
- Older employees are likely to have fewer financial responsibilities – their children are likely to be grown up, their mortgages may be paid off, etc.

ADVANTAGES FOR MANAGEMENT

- It may be easier to provide promotion opportunities for younger employees if older, more senior employees retire early.
- The use of this option in redundancy may mean that more difficult decisions about compulsory redundancy of younger employees can be avoided.

The early retirement option will not always be seen in such a rosy light. For management it is an expensive option because of the need to pay pensions early. In addition it cannot always be assumed that older employees have outdated skills and knowledge. In many cases such people's years of experience are of value to the organisation. Early retirement is usually voluntary. Thus management gives control of the selection process to employees. This may mean that the more useful older employees will leave whilst others whom management would wish to lose will stay.

In conclusion it is dangerous to generalise about people. Not all older employees are ready to retire. To attempt to encourage all this group to leave before normal retirement age is a superficially simple way of coping with redundancy. Good personnel practice would suggest that the needs of both the organisation and the individuals concerned must be carefully analysed before starting on this path.

Index

Nicki Stanton
The Business of Communicating
improving communication skills

Advice on the key elements of communication: writing letters, using the phone, interviewing, speaking in public. This book develops the principles explained in *What Do You Mean, 'Communication'?*. Coverage is geared to communication courses at BEC National and Higher levels whilst serving various other syllabus requirements: RSA Stage II, LCCI Intermediate, City & Guilds Communication Skills, foundation courses for professional examinations.

A Pan Breakthrough book, published in collaboration with the National Extension College.

David Floyd
Making Numbers Work
an introduction to business numeracy

A book to introduce the basic skills of business numeracy and explain how to apply them. An ideal text for the BEC General Module on Business Calculations, it also meets requirements of BEC National Module on Numeracy and Accounting, RSA Arithmetic Stages I, II and III and relevant parts of RSA Stage I Mathematics.

A Pan Breakthrough book, published in collaboration with the National Extension College.

Roger Oldcorn
Management
a fresh approach

A fresh introduction to the role of the modern manager. Coverage is geared to various syllabus requirements including the CNAA Diploma in Management Studies and those of the Institute of Industrial Management, Institute of Personnel Management, Institute of Purchasing and Supply and BEC Certificate in Management Studies courses.

A Pan Breakthrough book, published in collaboration with the National Extension College.

Terry Price
Practical Business Law

Pinpoints and explains the key areas of law which govern commercial life. The book is designed for use over a wide range of syllabuses: BEC General level Law and the Individual, BEC National level Organization in its Environment, RSA Stages II and III Commercial Law, LCCI Commercial Law syllabus higher stage, AEB O and A level Law, Oxford Local Examinations Board O and A level Law.

A Pan Breakthrough book, published in collaboration with the National Extension College.

John Etor and Mike Muspratt
Keep Account
a guide to profitable bookkeeping

Introduces and explains the basic principles of profitable bookkeeping. An ideal text for BEC General level Accounting, GCE O level Accounts and RSA Stage I bookkeeping syllabuses, it will also serve students on foundation courses for professional accounting qualifications.

A Pan Breakthrough book, published in collaboration with the National Extension College.

Peter Clark
Using Statistics in Business 1

Volume *1* shows how to acquire, judge and apply statistical information. Especially suitable for statistics courses at BEC National level in Numeracy and Accounting, RSA Stage II and LCCI Intermediate, it will also serve students of professional syllabuses: Institute of Chartered Accountants, Institute of Cost and Management Accountants, Institute of Chartered Secretaries, and Association of Certified Accountants.

A Pan Breakthrough book, published in collaboration with the National Extension College.

Using Statistics in Business 2

Volume *2* shows how to present and draw conclusions from statistical information. It develops the ideas explained in volume 1, and is especially suitable for statistics courses at BEC National level in Numeracy and Accounting, RSA Stage II and LCCI Intermediate. It will also serve students of professional syllabuses: Institute of Marketing, Institute of Personnel Management, Institute of Chartered Accountants, Institute of Cost and Management Accountants, Institute of Chartered Secretaries and Association of Certified Accountants.

A Pan Breakthrough book, published in collaboration with the National Extension College.

Reference, language and information

☐ **Pan Dictionary of Synonyms and Antonyms**		£1.95p
☐ **Travellers' Multilingual Phrasebook**		£1.95p
☐ **Universal Encyclopaedia of Mathematics**		£2.95p

Literature guides

☐ **An Introduction to Shakespeare and his Contemporaries**	Marguerite Alexander	£2.95p
☐ **An Introduction to Fifty American Poets**	Peter Jones	£1.75p
☐ **An Introduction to Fifty Modern British Plays**	Benedict Nightingale	£2.95p
☐ **An Introduction to Fifty American Novels**	Ian Ousby	£1.95p
☐ **An Introduction to Fifty British Novels 1600–1900**	Gilbert Phelps	£2.50p
☐ **An Introduction to Fifty Modern European Poets**	John Pilling	£2.95p
☐ **An Introduction to Fifty British Poets 1300–1900**	Michael Schmidt	£1.95p
☐ **An Introduction to Fifty Modern British Poets**		£2.95p
☐ **An Introduction to Fifty European Novels**	Martin Seymour-Smith	£1.95p
☐ **An Introduction to Fifty British Plays 1660–1900**	John Cargill Thompson	£1.95p

All these books are available at your local bookshop or newsagent, or can be ordered direct from the publisher. Indicate the number of copies required and fill in the form below   11

....

Name_____
(Block letters please)

Address_____

_____

Send to CS Department, Pan Books Ltd, PO Box 40, Basingstoke, Hants
Please enclose remittance to the value of the cover price plus:
35p for the first book plus 15p per copy for each additional book ordered
to a maximum charge of £1.25 to cover postage and packing
Applicable only in the UK

While every effort is made to keep prices low, it is sometimes
necessary to increase prices at short notice. Pan Books reserve
the right to show on covers and charge new retail prices which
may differ from those advertised in the text or elsewhere

Management

☐	**Effective Leadership**	John Adair	£2.50p
☐	**Introducing Management**	Christopher, McDonald and Wills	£1.95p
☐	**The Effective Executive**	} Peter Drucker	£1.95p
☐	**Management**		£3.50p
☐	**Under New Management**	Tony Eccles	£2.95p
☐	**Back from the Brink**	Michael Edwardes	£2.95p
☐	**How to Double Your Profits**	John Fenton	£2.50p
☐	**Inside Business Law**	} David Field	£2.95p
☐	**Inside Employment Law**		£2.50p
☐	**How to Win Customers**	Heinz Goldmann	£2.95p
☐	**The Black Economy**	Arnold Heertje *et al.*	£1.95p
☐	**Managing People at Work**	John Hunt	£2.50p
☐	**Investment Appraisal for Managers**	Graham Mott	£1.95p
☐	**Managing With Computers**	Terry Rowan	£2.95p
☐	**Guide to Saving and Investment**	James Rowlatt	£2.50p
☐	**Reality of Management**	} Rosemary Stewart	£1.95p
☐	**Reality of Organisations**		£1.95p
☐	**How to Manage**	Ray Wild	£2.50p
☐	**Bargaining for Results**	John Winkler	£1.95p
☐	**Dictionary of Economics and Commerce**		£1.50p
☐	**Multilingual Commercial Dictionary**		£3.95p

All these books are available at your local bookshop or newsagent, or
can be ordered direct from the publisher. Indicate the number of copies
required and fill in the form below   11
....

Name_____
(Block letters please)

Address_____

_____

Send to CS Department, Pan Books Ltd, PO Box 40, Basingstoke, Hants
Please enclose remittance to the value of the cover price plus:
35p for the first book plus 15p per copy for each additional book ordered
to a maximum charge of £1.25 to cover postage and packing
Applicable only in the UK

While every effort is made to keep prices low, it is sometimes
necessary to increase prices at short notice. Pan Books reserve
the right to show on covers and charge new retail prices which
may differ from those advertised in the text or elsewhere